BIRDS OF
LAND BETWEEN THE LAKES

Text by
David H. Snyder

Photography by
Frederick J. Alsop, III

❄❄❄❄❄❄❄

Additional photographs by

G. Ronald Austing
and
David H. Snyder

❄❄❄❄❄❄❄

Miscellaneous Publications of

The Center for Field Biology
Austin Peay State University
Clarksville, Tennessee 37044

Number 5   September 1991

FRONT COVER: Seven fledgling Belted Kingfishers, just out of their nest burrow, survey the outside world. Though they must soon feed themselves, they seem to be waiting for one more meal from Mom and Dad, or at least a quick lesson in fishing techniques.

BACK COVER: Land Between The Lakes is a 300 square mile recreation, education, and research facility administered by the Tennessee Valley Authority. Established in 1964 just before the impoundment of Lake Barkley, the area is heavily forested. An extensive system of roads, trails, campgrounds, and special visitor attractions makes it a haven for people wanting to get close to nature. For more information contact: Land Between The Lakes, Golden Pond, KY 42231 (phone: 502/924-5602).

Copyright © 1991 by Austin Peay State University

First published 1991 by The Center for Field Biology, Austin Peay State University, Clarksville, TN 37044

Library of Congress Catalog Card Number: 91-76141

ISBN 1-880617-00-5

Printed by Vaughan Printing, Nashville, TN

To my parents,
Pearl and Wallace Snyder.
For their love, their example, and their unflagging support.

To my wife,
Cathy.
For her strength, her goodness, her wit, and her taste.

And to my children,
Dianne, Brian, Nathan, Kathy, Shawn,
Isabelle,
Jared, Megan, and Logan.
For the joy, the wonder, and the memories.

David H. Snyder

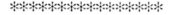

To the memory of
James T. Tanner, Ph.D.,
my major professor at the
University of Tennessee, Knoxville.

And to the faculty of
the APSU Department of Biology,
who made learning so exciting in my undergraduate years.

Fred J. Alsop, III

PREFACE

This book is the latest in a series of volumes produced by the Department of Biology at Austin Peay State University. Earlier volumes treated such subjects as lichens and ferns, amphibians and reptiles, spring wildflowers, summer and fall wildflowers, and trees of Land Between The Lakes (LBL).

As in the case of those earlier volumes, this one—on the birds of LBL—is intended to serve as an introduction to the study and enjoyment of a single portion of the broad spectrum of natural history subjects that present themselves to the visitor in LBL. The target audience is the beginner who has little knowledge of the birds of the region but wants to learn, although experienced birders (jargon for "bird watchers") may find some useful information here. This book is not intended to substitute for the several excellent guides to the field identification of the area's birds which are currently available on the market (see the bibliography for a list of these and other publications which the reader may find useful). But considerable information on how to recognize species is included, especially for the more common forms, to give the budding birder a taste of the joys and challenges of bird identification. Except for the descriptions, the species accounts are largely anecdotal, emphasizing things which I find interesting about each species, and which I am presumptuous enough to expect the reader might also find interesting.

The number of bird species reliably reported as occurring in or near LBL exceeds 250, but only about one-fourth that number are common or abundant in LBL during at least one season of the year. Several species have been reported only once or a very few times, and are unlikely to be encountered. The whole subject of status and abundance categories for birds is a bit confusing as encountered in the ornithological literature, and I include in the introduction a summary of my view and simplified treatment of that subject in this work.

The color photographs illustrating this book are mostly the work of Fred Alsop. Ron Austing has supplied most of those not made by Fred. Since most of the photographs were not made in LBL, some of the plant species seen in the photographs do not occur there, and in several cases the photographs are of individual birds doing things which their species is not known to do in LBL—specifically, nesting. Photographs at the nest, of species which are not known to nest in LBL, are noted in the caption accompanying the photograph.

ACKNOWLEDGMENTS

This book owes much to the flocks of ornithologists who have preceded me and recorded much of what they learned in various books and periodicals. I have consulted those publications freely and used much information from them, usually without attribution. But I am aware of and hereby acknowledge my indebtedness to them.

Several organizations and individuals deserve specific acknowledgment for assistance in the preparation of this work. Austin Peay State University's Center for Field Biology provided logistical and financial support. Tennessee Valley Authority personnel stationed at Land Between The Lakes were supportive in many ways. Throughout the six year gestation of the book Ben Stone was a constant, gentle, and effective prod toward completion of the project. Clell Peterson, emeritus professor of Murray State University, has contributed immensely to our knowledge of the birds of LBL. John Robinson and Donald Blunk deserve specific mention for their study of the birds of LBL, especially those of the southern portion of the area. Michael Dinsmore, Dave Easterla, Todd Easterla, Rick Phillips, and Damien Simbeck, all of whom have worked with me on studies of the forest breeding birds of LBL, have graciously provided me with comments on their observations of the summer birds of LBL. Amy Bishop helped with the literature research. Gwen Sunderland, Julie Brash, Ed Irwin, and Fred Alsop all read the manuscript, and their comments have resulted in a substantially more accurate and readable product. Surely errors remain, and they are mine.

David H. Snyder
August 1991

CONTENTS

INTRODUCTION

Description of the Area

An area such as Land Between The Lakes provides a wonderful place in which to get close to nature. That is, after all, one of the major purposes for which the facility was established in 1964. The three hundred square miles that comprise LBL occupy a peninsula of land astride a ridge separating the lower reaches of the drainages of the Tennessee and Cumberland rivers. The peninsula's long axis (about 40 miles) trends north-northwest to south-southeast. The average width of the peninsula is about seven miles. Parts of three counties—Stewart, in Tennessee, and Trigg and Lyon in Kentucky—accommodate the national recreation area.

Within LBL there are several types of habitat, occupying sites from the lake margins up to the crests of the dry ridges separating the various watersheds in the area. Normal lake level is about 359 feet above sea level, with seasonal variation reflecting the vagaries of weather and the regulation of lake levels to accommodate hydroelectric power generation, flood control, navigation, and so on. In the Kentucky portion of LBL the Tennessee-Cumberland drainage divide occurs generally along the line described by The Trace, the major north-south roadway in LBL (in Tennessee, The Trace lies mostly in the Cumberland drainage). Though the relief in LBL is slight—only about 300 feet (with the highest point in LBL being slightly over 660 feet above sea level)—the effects of soil moisture on vegetation can be striking, and soil moisture in LBL is generally inversely correlated with elevation. The ridgetop soils typically have poor moisture-retention capabilities, and plants occurring there must be able to withstand severe water stress during droughts.

Just as climatic and soil conditions have a major effect on the vegetation that occurs in an area, so does the vegetation affect the numbers and kinds of animals present (an oversimplification, of course, but valid as a general rule). Thus, one of the first lessons learned by anyone interested in the study of any natural community of animals is that animal communities reflect the plant communities in which they occur. Birds abide by this rule, so to see the greatest variety of birds, watchers must visit the greatest variety of plant communities that they can find.

But just what is a plant community, how many are there in LBL, and how can they be distinguished from one another? Good, relevant questions, but questions with no simple answers. Chester and Ellis (see bibliography) have devised a plant community classification scheme for the LBL region, and readers may find it rewarding to consult their paper. But birders needn't get too technical with this sort of thing; if two areas look different in terms of the plants present, then probably the differences will also be detectable to the birds. The idea is to check as many different kinds of habitats as possible, in order to see as many different kinds of birds as possible.

Man has substantially altered the habitats of LBL since his arrival in the area in significant numbers just a couple of hundred years ago. At the time of the first white settlers in the late eighteenth century, virgin forests covered essentially the entire area (though a few scattered patches of prairie may have been present). But even then the forest was doubtless not homogeneous from riverside to ridgetop. Species of plants and animals occurred then which don't now; among trees, for example, the magnificent American chestnut—though probably never a dominant species in LBL forests—has all but disappeared from the area because of a blight introduced into this country from Europe during the early decades of this century. Essentially all of the virgin forest of LBL was cut in the 1800s and used as fuel for firing the furnaces of the local iron industry, for sawtimber, for railroad crosstie production, and for domestic use on the homesteads in the area. Today there are no virgin stands of timber left in LBL.

Among animals, the Passenger Pigeon, one of the most abundant species of birds the world has ever seen, was a major consumer of the mast crop produced by the trees of the virgin forests in LBL; it is now extinct, and whatever effects the activities of such vast flocks of birds may have had on the forest communities of LBL are now, and forever will be, gone. Cougar, black bear, timber wolf, and wild bison are also gone.

Though it is impossible not to notice the disappearance

4

from an area of such species as these, it is very possible not to notice the disappearance of "lesser" species which, by virtue of their smaller numbers, size, or impact on man's enterprises are lost before they are ever "found." But nature is nothing if not dynamic. The addition and deletion of the ingredients in an ecological system and the changing of proportions of those ingredients are not only typical, but probably inevitable in nature. The evolutionary process ensures that. Yet we are witness to, and the primary cause of, an accelerated rate of species extinction unparalleled in the last 65 million years—since the disappearance of the dinosaurs. And measured against the standards set by those 65 thousand millenia, the breakneck pace of species extinctions that exists today is anything but typical.

Species Accounts

The 230 species treated in this book represent a personal selection from among more than 250 species that have either been recorded for LBL or that I believe, based on what is known of their status in surrounding areas, might reasonably be expected to occur there. Some species which have been reported from LBL are not included because of their extreme rarity in the region.

The sequence of the accounts in this book may perplex the beginner. It follows the order established by the American Ornithologists' Union (see bibliography). Though not universally used in field guides, it is commonly used, and has the advantage over other systems of reflecting something of what we know about relationships among birds. So Chimney Swift and Ruby-throated Hummingbird are juxtaposed because they are more closely related to each other than either is to any other species in LBL. And Loggerhead Shrike, though it looks and acts like a small hawk, is found among the songbirds. Thus the sequence, apparently nonsensical, is really quite sensible, and there is something to be learned by paying attention to it.

Every species account includes:

Names. Both scientific and common (or vernacular) names are given, as sanctioned by the American Ornithologists' Union's Check-list of North American Birds (6th ed.), and supplements through 1990.

Size. The sizes given have been compiled from several standard sources, and represent length from bill tip to tail tip, with the bird lying on its back, neck and head extended. The sizes are averages for the species, but most individuals will be within 10% of the given size; American Robin for example, listed at 10 inches, may be anywhere from 9 to 11 inches, whereas Common Yellowthroat, listed at 5 inches, may be anywhere from 4.5 to 5.5 inches. American Robins, therefore, are larger *on average* than Hairy Woodpeckers (listed at 9 inches), but a large Hairy Woodpecker may be larger than a small American Robin. In species with males and females of markedly different sizes, average figures for each sex are given.

Residency status. The "residency status" of a species in an area refers to its seasonality of occurrence, breeding, and occurrence within or outside of its established range. Birds are unusually mobile animals, and some of them undergo impressive movements between points on the earth's surface, usually on an annual cycle. These movements, called migrations, result in a dynamic pattern of change in the list of species present in LBL at different times of the year. For the sake of describing the annual pattern of change that characterizes the occurrence of a particular species in a particular area, a classification scheme has been developed by ornithologists and, inevitably, an accompanying terminology. The categories in that scheme are called residency status categories. The following definitions and discussions of those categories, though simplified, should allow an understanding of the information provided in the species accounts.

Permanent resident. Species which occur throughout the year. The fact that a species occurs year-round does not mean necessarily that the same individual birds are present year-round. In the case of most permanent residents in LBL, we do not know the extent to which individual birds are entering and leaving the area seasonally. It does not follow, therefore, that a permanent species in LBL is a nonmigratory species. Common Grackles, for example, are permanent residents in LBL, though we are certain that many, perhaps most, of the Common Grackles found in LBL in January nest far to the north.

6

Summer resident. Species which are absent in the dead of winter, but are present during the season when breeding occurs. Though most of these species breed in LBL, a few do not (e.g., Snowy Egret). In those cases where a summer resident is not a breeding species in LBL, the individual birds present during the breeding season may be nonbreeding birds (this usually means that the bird is sexually immature; some species require more than one year to reach sexual maturity), or they may be birds that are nesting outside LBL but are visiting to forage (e.g., probably most Chimney Swifts seen in LBL do not nest there—there are few chimneys left in LBL—but this wide-ranging species, which spends hours aloft and flies many miles daily, is common in LBL's summer skies).

Winter resident. Species which nest north of LBL and come south to LBL to spend their winters.

Transient. Species which pass through LBL as they are migrating north to their breeding grounds in the spring or south to their wintering grounds in the fall. Though all transients are migrants, not all migrants are transients; the distinction, though obvious upon reflection, is sometimes ignored by people who use these two terms interchangeably. Actually, migratory species occur in all of the residency status groups including, as explained earlier, the permanent resident group.

We traditionally subdivide the year into four seasons. Astronomically, those seasons are based on the solstices and the equinoxes. But the recognition of four seasons is of course arbitrary. We could as logically recognize two, or eight, or twelve. If we choose to recognize four, how do we assign the months? June in LBL is surely summer to most birds (at least I assume it would be, if they were to concern themselves with such matters); yet astronomically most of June is spring. What is March in LBL? Astronomically, mostly winter, but biologically, mostly spring. Of course one could ignore the astronomical definitions of the seasons and use biological ones instead. For example, restricting our consideration of biology to that of birds (please pardon the chauvinism), we could define summer as that time of year when birds court, mate, build nests, lay and incubate eggs, and raise young. Or we might want to drop the courting and mating part and date the beginning of summer as the beginning of nest building. Spring could be defined as the time when transients pass through LBL on their way north, and fall the time when they come back through headed south. Winter would be what's left over. If we then wanted to assign the months to the seasons defined thusly, beginning with January, we would call it winter, right? Well, it depends.... Some owls may already be incubating eggs in late January in LBL. American Goldfinches, on the other hand, may not begin egg laying until July. In the case of species which rear more than one brood per season (e.g., Mourning Dove and Eastern Bluebird, both of which may rear three broods in a season), then summer as defined above would occupy half or more of the calendar year. You see the problem: nature is cavalierly unsympathetic and uncooperative with our human insistence on dissecting and pigeonholing her.

To accommodate the many and unsynchronized patterns of occurrence of the 230 species of birds that are treated in this book, I have therefore defined the seasons for each species according to its particular pattern of occurrence in LBL. Thus, Pied-billed Grebe is called a winter resident even though it is regularly found there in all months except June and July. Yet its abundance changes noticeably during the period of its residency in LBL. It is fairly common until December, then uncommon through February, and then fairly common again from March through May as individual birds which have spent the deepest part of the winter further south visit LBL on their northward migration. By June the species is typically not to be found in LBL (though there are a few summer records). Taking Spotted Sandpiper as another example, I list it as a summer resident. From April through May it is fairly common and most (possibly all) of the birds in LBL at this time are northbound migrants. I know of no June records of Spotted Sandpiper from LBL. In July the species becomes fairly common again and remains so well into October. In the absence of any June records, one might wonder why I categorize it as a summer resident instead of as a spring and fall transient. The reason is that several June records, including some nesting records, exist for the species in many parts of Tennessee, well to the south of its main breeding range (which extends northward from northern Kentucky). Considering those June records, several from near LBL, and given the presence in LBL of what appears to be suitable breeding habitat, it seems reasonable to place Spotted Sandpiper in the summer resident category. Wishful thinking perhaps, but at least a modicum of supporting logic. Similar considerations were made in the cases of many other species regarding their residency status and abundance in LBL. Surely other experienced birders will disagree with some of my decisions regarding the assignment of species to particular residency status and abundance categories, and I even find myself second-guessing myself in some instances. But so long as we persist in imposing discrete categories onto data which is not only a continuum, but imperfect, such problems will be with us.

In summary, it may be easier for the reader to think of residency status category assignments as being based on knowledge of if and when a species is *absent* from LBL, and the seasonality of that absence. That perspective results in the following definitions of the four residency status categories used in this book:

Permanent resident. The species is normally not absent during any part of any season.

Summer resident. The species is normally absent during at least part of the cold season.

Winter resident. The species is normally absent during at least part of the warm season.

Transient. The species is normally absent during two distinct periods, once during the warm season and once during the cold season.

Although this view of the system is conceptually assailable (e.g., it does not result in the proper assignment of a species which passes through an area during its spring migration, but not during its fall migration) it will nonetheless work with almost all of the species treated in this book.

Abundance. Abundance of a species in an area refers to the number of individuals of, and frequency of encounters with, that species that may be expected by an experienced birder searching conscientiously in the proper habitat within the species' established range. I have used five abundance categories in this book. The allocation of species among those categories was sometimes a subjective exercise, and is intended to serve only as an estimate of the probability that a species will be recorded by an experienced birder searching conscientiously in the appropriate habitat at the right time of year. The category assignments of the species are based on my personal experience birding in and around LBL for nearly 30 years, and my interpretation of the published literature. Other birders, with as much experience and with access to the same literature, would almost surely make different assignments in many cases. It is also true that species may change in abundance with the passing years (several instances of that are mentioned in the species accounts; Bewick's Wren, Blue Grosbeak, and Cliff Swallow are just a few examples). Plant community successional changes that are occurring as much of LBL reverts toward pristineness, land management practices in and around LBL, species restoration projects, climatic changes, severe weather events, destruction of the tropical rain forests where many of LBL's transients and summer residents spend their winters, and doubtless many other factors continue to affect the abundance of many bird species in LBL. So the abundance category assignments represent, at best, one man's educated guess at the current situation. The best analysis of the subject of abundance categories for birds of which I am aware is provided in the introduction of DeSante and Pyle (see bibliography). The abundance categories I have used are based on their analysis, though I have simplified things a bit.

Common. Species which are encountered on 90% of birding trips by an experienced birder working appropriate habitat at the proper time of year.

Fairly common. Species encountered on 50-90% of trips.

Uncommon. Species encountered on 10-50% of trips.

Rare. Species encountered on 1-10% of trips.

Extremely rare. Species encountered on fewer than 1% of trips.

Basic description. The descriptions of the birds are

based on information found in several field guides, handbooks, technical and popular periodicals, and in many cases on examination of specimens in the Austin Peay State University Museum of Zoology. They are moderately complete in most cases, but not exhaustive. A few species, like American Crow, can be easily described in a single sentence for both sexes and all ages. But most species have more complex plumage patterns which often differ between the sexes, between breeding and nonbreeding seasons, and between immature and adult birds. The subject of plumages and molts in birds is too complicated to treat here. As a rule, I describe the breeding males first, and then females, immatures, and winter adults if they differ from the breeding males. In several cases the plumages are so complex that I have not tried to describe all their intricacies and variations, but have instead referred the reader to a field guide. Field guides are specifically designed as aids to field identification. Those listed in the bibliography of this book are all excellent and well-illustrated with paintings. To interpret the descriptions, one must know the names for the various areas of the bird's body (i.e., its topography). Many of these terms—such as head, wings, tail, and legs—are obvious. But others—e.g., nape, flanks, undertail coverts, speculum, and mantle—are not so generally known, and the reader should consult the labeled illustration of the topography of a bird on page 17, and the glossary, until the meanings of these terms are clear.

Other information provided for the many species varies. Usually some mention is made of preferred habitat and vocalizations. Food habits and nests are sometimes mentioned, but not regularly. Anecdotes on many species provide a sampling of the fascinating lives and lore of birds. The reader is strongly encouraged to dip into some of the excellent literature listed in the bibliography.

HOW TO WATCH BIRDS

Bird watching is one of the most popular recreational activities in America, and it grows more popular each year. It can be pursued casually or avidly. For some, it becomes an obsession—hard-core birders, we call them. Required equipment is minimal and includes a field guide, binocular, pencil, and notebook.

A binocular is indispensable for any but the most casual birding, and is to a birder what a fielder's glove is to a shortstop; you could play the game without one, but why would you want to. Before investing in a binocular, learn something about binoculars in general—talk with an experienced birder or check out a book from the library. *Don't* rely on the advice of a salesperson (unless you *know* that person to be aware of both the basics of binocular design and construction, and the specific needs of birders in a binocular). And though you needn't splurge in buying a binocular, neither should you buy cheap. Birding is hard on a binocular, and one that gives what appears to be a clear, bright image in the showroom is likely not to hold up well if it is shoddily made.

At least as important as image quality is optical alignment. If the light paths of the two separate optical systems that comprise a binocular are not aligned well, the user may see a double image. If the misalignment is less serious, the viewer's eyes will attempt to "correct" the misalignment by a sort of compensatory realignment of the eyes themselves; though this correction may result in the perception of a single image, the exertion of the eye muscles is tiring and may result in headaches and eyestrain. Cheaply made binoculars are very prone to misalignment resulting from even minor jarring, and the cost of realignment may exceed the purchase price of the binocular.

The power of magnification should be between 6 and 10. The lower powers are better for beginners and for watching nearby, active birds in heavy cover. With experience, and for viewing more distant birds in more open areas, the higher powers may be better. A strong, comfortable neck strap is an excellent idea, and that strap should always be used; sooner or later you will drop the binocular, and the strap will save the day (and maybe your foot).

Using a binocular is a bit like using a gun—to be effective, it must be aimed properly and held steady. A common frustration of beginning birders is to spy a bird with the naked eye, whip the binocular up to see it better, and not be able to find it in the field of view. Practice helps. Another aid is to note the position of the bird in relation to conspicuous features in your field of vision before you put the binocular to your eyes. For example, a bird in a tree may be on the second large limb up, on the left, two-thirds of the way out from the trunk. So, find the base of the trunk through your binocular, follow the trunk up to the second large limb on the left, pan left two-thirds of the way to the branch tips, and hope the bird hasn't moved while you were doing all this.

Two hands are required to shoot a rifle properly, and two hands are required to use a binocular to best advantage. One of the best field marks for identifying beginning birders is their habit of holding a bird book in one hand, a binocular in the other, and glancing back and forth between the two, frantically trying to identify the bird before it moves on. The problem with that technique is that it takes two hands to hold and flip the pages of the book, and two hands to properly hold the binocular (it's not that the binocular is too heavy for one-handed use, but that the image is too unsteady—too jerky: an 8-power binocular magnifies not only the image 8 times—64 times in terms of area—but vibrations as well). A different analysis might conclude the problem to be that we don't have four hands. Regardless of the cause of the problem, the solution is simple: use two hands to hold the binocular, take mental notes of what you see, then commit your binocular to its neck strap and use two hands on your book. But what to do with your book when both hands are supporting your binocular? Something. Anything. Slip it in a jacket pocket or book holster, tuck it under your belt, hold it between your legs, lay it down on something nearby, or have your secretary hold it open to the proper section and flip pages as directed. But get it out of your hands when using your binocular.

Regarding the point about taking mental notes of what you see as you view the bird, it is obvious I suppose that it helps to have some idea of what features you should be taking note of. The breast? The undertail coverts? The color of the iris? The proportionate size of the bill? The presence or absence of an eye-ring? Learning such esoterica is a big part of the labor of love that birding is to so many, and what field guides are designed to facilitate. Study of your field guide when you're not in the field will yield rewards later, though I am convinced that no learning sticks with you like that which occurs under the euphoric duress of the field.

A pencil and notebook should be part of the equipment of every birder, though I confess that my position on this point is colored by my long experience as a field biologist and teacher. Of course it's possible to watch and enjoy birds without ever taking a written note. But memories fade, mingle, and mutate, whereas written records do not. Field ornithology is justly famous for the contributions of its amateurs to the discipline, and accurate, detailed, disciplined field notes are at the core of those contributions. But aside from that, it is simply fun for many birders, in later years or when cabin fever strikes, to relive earlier field trips by reading their accounts of them. And taking notes will almost surely make you more observant; after all, you can't write in detail about what you've seen if you don't observe carefully.

BIRDING "HOT SPOTS"

Within LBL there is decent birding nearly everywhere. But some areas are particularly good because of the conjunction of habitat types. The Environmental Education Area surrounding Hematite Lake, Honker Lake, and the Woodlands Nature Center, astride the Trigg-Lyon county border in the Cumberland River drainage is one of my favorite spots. A nice trail encircles Hematite Lake, and by taking it one can encounter water birds, forest birds, swamp birds (in the Barnes Hollow area where it joins the headwaters of Hematite Lake), and birds that prefer semiopen, parklike areas (adjacent to and below the spillway). Also in the area is the Silo Overlook (just south of the Youth Station) that provides a commanding view of Lake Barkley. A couple of miles south of Hematite Lake is Energy Lake, which also has a good system of trails around it.

The developed campgrounds in LBL, the welcome stations, Golden Pond Visitors' Center, The Homeplace-1850, Brandon Spring Group Camp, and many of the lake access sites provide good birding, especially for species that like semiopen sites. Beaver ponds exist at several places in LBL, and the marshlands and wooded swamps that they produce are excellent habitat for several species of birds. The locations of the beaver ponds tend to change with the passing years, but TVA personnel should be able to tell you where some good ones are at the time of your visit. The many miles of roads in LBL are mostly accessible to the public (pick up a free map at the welcome station, visitors' center, etc., that will show you precisely which roads are "legal" in the year of your visit) and can carry you from lakeside to ridgetop, and to many kinds of habitat.

There are some excellent birding areas outside of but near LBL which the reader may want to take advantage of. Kentucky and Barkley dams, on the Tennessee River and Cumberland River, respectively, are just north of LBL, and are "hot spots" for various waterbirds (loons, grebes, diving ducks, gulls) that like large, deep bodies of water, or the tailwaters below the dams. The areas both above and below those dams are excellent, especially in winter.

Just south of LBL there are also some good birding

spots. Cross Creeks National Wildlife Refuge is 3 miles south of Dover, Tennessee. It consists of almost 9000 acres of the Cumberland River floodplain and adjacent hills. Established in 1962, primarily as a waterfowl refuge, it has become one of the best birding areas in the region. The article by Robinson and Blunk (see bibliography) provides a good account of birding opportunities at Cross Creeks National Wildlife Refuge and several other areas in Stewart County, Tennessee.

Just west of Kentucky Lake at the southwest corner of LBL is Paris Landing State Park—a good spot for migrating and wintering waterbirds. The open water is expansive there, and a spotting scope is a real help. Some three miles south of the bridge over Kentucky Lake at Paris Landing is Pace Point, at the northern tip of the Big Sandy Unit of Tennessee National Wildlife Refuge. Pace Point is at the tip of the peninsula separating the Big Sandy and Tennessee rivers, and is peerless as an area for finding rare shorebirds in the LBL region. Though less than 4 miles from LBL as the loon swims, it is about 10 times that distance by road. Mid-July to mid-September is the best time to visit Pace Point for shorebirds, but May is also good. The book by Bierly (see bibliography) gives explicit instructions, with maps, on how to get to these and other attractive birding spots in Tennessee, and lists many of the "feature attraction" birds at each site.

BIRD TOPOGRAPHY

The reader may be unfamiliar with some of the terms used in the species accounts to describe birds. The illustration below includes many of these terms, and several others are defined in the glossary. Since the terms are used so frequently, it's a good idea for the beginning birder to learn them as quickly as possible.

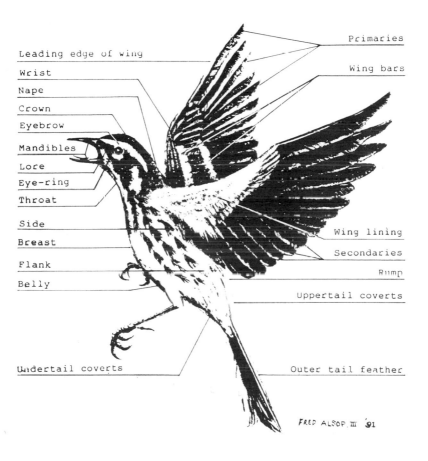

Leading edge of wing
Wrist
Nape
Crown
Eyebrow
Mandibles
Lore
Eye-ring
Throat
Side
Breast
Flank
Belly
Undertail coverts

Primaries
Wing bars
Wing lining
Secondaries
Rump
Uppertail coverts
Outer tail feather

FRED ALSOP III '91

SPECIES ACCOUNTS

Common Loon *Gavia immer* 32 in.
Uncommon winter (Oct. to mid-May) resident.

Common Loon is a large water bird with a strong, sharply pointed, dark bill. Breeding adults have a glossy, black or greenish-black head and neck, with a black-and-white-striped partial collar low on the neck. The upperparts are otherwise basically black, with attractive grid-like arrangements of squarish, white spots and smaller, round white spots. The underparts behind the throat are mostly pure white. Immatures and winter birds, which are the plumages most commonly seen in LBL, are dark gray above, whitish below. Distant loons resemble cormorants but may be distinguished from them by silhouette; loons have sharp-pointed (rather than hooked) bills, and the bill tends to be held with its long axis nearly parallel with the water's surface (in cormorants, the bill tends to be tilted skyward slightly). Excellent swimmers and divers, Common Loons are also strong fliers, though they need a long "runway" for takeoffs and landings. In flight Common Loon's neck and head droop below the body's major axis, giving the bird a "hunchbacked" look; the trailing, dangling legs and feet accentuate this effect. On land, where they are almost never seen except at the nest, they are truly awkward. Look for Common Loon on large, open expanses of water. Its call is one of the great sounds of nature, variously described as yodeling, or maniacal laughing; it also makes a long, haunting "ha-oooooo" call. It eats mostly fish and aquatic invertebrates.

Pied-billed Grebe *Podilymbus podiceps* 13 in.   **p.155**
Winter resident. Fairly common fall (mid-Aug. through Nov.) and spring (March through May); uncommon winter.

A small (pigeon-sized), extremely short-tailed, chicken-billed water bird, with lobed (instead of webbed) toes. Excellent swimmers and divers, they are rarely seen on land. Breeding adults are mostly brownish gray, with a whitish patch beneath the tail, a black throat patch, white eye-ring, and white bill that bears a black ring at midlength. Winter

18

birds (see photograph) are browner, with an unringed, pale bill, and light throat. Fond of ponds, marshes, and nearshore lake waters, often where there is aquatic vegetation. While swimming, may deflate its lungs and compress its feathers until its body submerges, leaving only its head and neck exposed, periscope-like. Takeoff requires a good stretch of water, where it "patters" along the surface with its feet as it gains enough speed to become fully airborne. The call is impressive and loud, beginning fast and then gradually slowing down, a rather hollow-sounding "kow-kow-kow-kow, kow, kow, kow, kowp, kowp, kowp." Usually seen singly, or in small groups.

Horned Grebe *Podiceps auritus* 13½ in.
Uncommon winter (Oct. through May) resident.

Breeding adults (not likely to be seen in LBL) are blackish above, with a chestnut neck, breast, and sides. The head, throat, and bill are basically black, but it has large, yellowish ear tufts ("horns"), and blood-red eyes. In flight the large, white patch is visible on the trailing half of each inner wing. Winter birds are white on the underparts, dark gray above. The top half of the head (from the eye up) and the back of the neck are black. The lower half of the head is white. The bill of Horned Grebe is longer and less chicken-like than in Pied-billed Grebe. Though the two regular grebes of LBL are nearly the same size, Horned Grebe occurs more on deeper waters of the large lakes, where it is a consummate diver.It requires a long "runway" for takeoff. As a grebe, of course, it has lobed rather than webbed toes. It feeds on fish and aquatic invertebrates. They are quite silent on their wintering grounds.

Double-crested Cormorant *Phalacrocorax auritus* 31 in.
Winter resident. Uncommon fall (Sept. through Nov.) and spring (March through May); rare winter.

A large water bird, this relative of the pelicans resembles Common Loon in appearance more than any other bird of LBL. Plumage of breeding adults usually appears solid black, but up close in good light there is a greenish-to-purplish iridescence above. The bill is black, rather slender, and bears a hawk-like hook at its tip. The throat pouch and face in front of the eyes are yellow, the legs and feet are black, and the toes are fully webbed. Two tufts of feathers at the sides of the crown are usually not apparent. Immatures are brown above, paler below, and may have mostly yellow bills. Excellent swimmers and divers, and strong fliers, Double-crested Cormorants can usually be distinguished from Common Loons on the water by the slightly upward tilt at which the bill is held, and the hook at its tip. In flight, Double-crested Cormorant appears to have a lump in its throat (because the neck is not fully extended), and the head is carried slightly above the body's major axis. They often fly in formations, like geese. Unlike loons, cormorants often alight on posts, towers, dead trees, etc., near water, where they have a rather erect stance, necessitated by the position of the legs so far back on the body. They feed mostly on fish, and are silent (except at the nest).

American Bittern *Botaurus lentiginosus* 25 in.
Rare spring (mid-March to late May) and fall (Sept. through Nov.) transient.

This lover of tall, dense, marsh vegetation is a fairly large heron (about the size of Red-tailed Hawk). The upperparts are mottled and streaked in various shades of brown, and the throat and breast are boldly streaked with rufous and white (or buff). The flight feathers are blackish, and in flight contrast sharply with the warm brown of the rest of the wing. Adults have a long, black patch on each side of the neck, and greenish legs. American Bittern stalks the cattail marshes and grassy swamps, looking for any animal it can subdue for food. Frogs, snakes, insects, and small mammals are all taken. One of the more descriptive common names for this bird is "thunder pumper," based on its eerie, hollow call, usually heard at night or twilight, coming from the swamp: "oong ga-chunk, oong ga-chunk, oong ga-chunk, oong ga-chunk." That marvelous sound is rarely if ever heard in LBL, however, where they are not known to breed. As a passive defense against intruders, they often "freeze" among the reeds, facing the interloper, bill pointed to the heavens; it is astonishing how such a large bird can thus—given the right combination of habitat, appearance, and behavior—"melt" into nothingness before your eyes. When flushed, a low "kok-kok-kok" may be uttered.

Least Bittern *Ixobrychus exilis* 12½ in.

Summer resident. Rare spring (mid-April through May) and fall (Aug. through Sept); extremely rare summer.

A small, secretive heron of dense, emergent, aquatic vegetation. Adult males are black on the back and crown. The wings above show dark flight feathers, and a prominent buff patch (bordered behind by chestnut) on the inner forewing. The underparts are yellowish-buff, streaked with white, and the side of the face and neck show much rufous. Bill, legs, and feet are yellowish. Females and immatures are similar, but have chestnut crowns and backs, and streaked throats. Though likely to "freeze" instead of flush when approached in their natural element, they can fly. When they do flush, the flight seems feeble, as they barely clear the vegetation, legs dangling, before dropping into the jungle again just a few yards away. When they freeze with heads up and gaze forward, they are almost invisible. But if you can spot them, it may be possible (as I did once) to approach them cautiously and drop a butterfly net over them, they are so confident of their invisibility. They are quite acrobatic as they move gracefully among the reeds and cattails, grasping the stems with their long toes. Their diet consists of small marsh animals. The call is a series of three or four soft, low "coo" notes, similar to Black-billed Cuckoo's song.

Great Blue Heron *Ardea herodias* 48 in.   **p.155**
Common permanent resident.

The largest heron of LBL, and the largest bird of any kind in LBL if you measure size by total length; with neck extended (as it usually is not), it is nearly four feet long, and in flight it sports a six-foot wingspan. Though often called cranes by local residents, herons are not even closely related to the true cranes (appearances can be deceiving). Adults (see photograph) are bluish-gray on the back and on the visible portions of the folded wings. The sides and back of the long neck are gray, the throat white with black stripes. The white head has two broad, black stripes above the eyes, the black continuing to the tips of two plumes that emerge from the back of the head. The breast and back are also fringed with plumelike feather extensions. The breast is black-and-white striped, the belly black, the thighs chestnut, and the legs grayish. A powerful, long, yellow, sharp-pointed bill is used, forceps-fashion, to catch frogs, fish, snakes, etc., which are patiently stalked and then captured with a quick thrust of the head. The dark gray flight feathers contrast, in flight, with the blue-gray of the rest of the wing. Juveniles lack plumes and are grayer above. Great Blue Heron occurs in nearly all wetland environments of LBL, from streamsides to lakesides, and beaver ponds to farm ponds, often perching in trees. Normally silent, it sometimes gives a primeval squawk in flight or when flushed.

Great Egret *Casmerodius albus* 39 in.   **p.156**
Uncommon summer (mid-March to mid-Nov.) resident.

A large, long-legged, long-necked, all-white wading bird, with a heavy yellow bill and black legs and feet. In breeding plumage (see photograph), long, delicate plumes cascade from the breast and lower back. Immatures are similar, but lack the plumes, and have a dark tip to the bill. As a typical heron (rather than a true crane), Great Egret flies with its neck flexed in a loop rather than extended, though during takeoffs and landings it may extend its neck; thus in flight, herons, bitterns, and egrets look shorter-necked than they often do standing. The call is a sort of croak, but this species seldom calls away from the nest. Though described here as a summer resident, they do not commonly nest in LBL (In 1989 a single nest was found in a Black-crowned Night-Heron rookery on Lake Barkley). Like many herons they are colonial nesters. From around 10 to thousands of nesting pairs may occur in a colony, and such concentrations of large birds are conspicuous. Great Egrets may be seen in LBL at any time during the summer months, but these may be nonbreeding birds, or birds that have completed their breeding elsewhere and have then dispersed to nonbreeding areas (sometimes far to the north of their nesting areas) to feed before heading south for the winter. Birds exhibiting such post-nesting dispersal into areas outside both their usual breeding and wintering ranges are called "summer visitants" in areas like LBL, and several species of herons and egrets commonly exhibit such behavior.

Snowy Egret *Egretta thula* 24 in.
Rare summer (mid-April through Aug.) resident.

Nearly as large as Little Blue Heron, this species has solid white plumage, with a black bill, and yellow lores and eyes. The black legs (immatures may have a yellowish stripe on the back of the leg), sharply contrasting yellow feet (muddy feet of course may be mud-colored), and black bill distinguish Snowy Egret from Cattle Egret and Great Egret (see account of Little Blue Heron for tips on distinguishing immatures of that species from Snowy Egret). Marshes, ponds, wooded swamps, and lake margins are the usual habitats for this species. In breeding plumage the filmy plumes on the head, back, and neck are quite spectacular. Snowy Egret was one of the primary targets of the commercial plume hunters who decimated heron rookeries over much of North America around the turn of the century to procure adornments for women's hats. Since protective legislation was passed, this and several other heron species have recovered well and now occur in areas where they did not before the plume hunting era. They have also benefitted from the 1972 ban on the insecticide DDT. Snowy Egret is not known to breed in or near LBL.

Little Blue Heron *Egretta caerulea* 25 in. **p.156**
Uncommon summer (April to mid-Oct.) resident.

This medium-sized heron as an adult (see photograph) is basically slate blue all over, except for a brownish-purple head and neck. The bill is bluish toward its base, with a black tip. The legs and feet are dark, greenish-blue to nearly black. Immature birds have solid white plumage (except for dark wing tips), and are essentially the same size as the all-white Snowy Egret. A good look at the bill, or legs and feet, however, will allow discrimination: immature Little Blue Herons have a bluish bill with a black tip (compared with solid black in Snowy Egret), and dull, yellowish-green legs and feet (compared with black legs and yellow feet in Snowy). The other two species of white, long-legged waders in LBL (Great Egret and Cattle Egret) have yellow or coral bills. Little Blues which are changing from immature to adult plumage have a pied look (blotched blue and white). Little Blue Herons have recently nested in Trigg County, Kentucky, on an island in Lake Barkley, but probably many Little Blue Herons seen in LBL in late summer and fall are summer visitants, having bred elsewhere earlier in the year. Beaver ponds and similar wet-and-wooded locations are favored haunts of Little Blue Heron in LBL, but it will also patrol mudflats and marshes. It feeds largely on fish, but takes other vertebrates and invertebrates as well.

Cattle Egret *Bubulcus ibis* 20 in.
Uncommon summer (early April through Oct.) resident.

The plumage of this crow-sized bird is entirely white, except that breeding birds have buffish-orange plumes on their crowns, backs, and lower throats. The bill, legs, and feet of breeding birds are coral (nonbreeding adults and immatures have yellow bills and yellow to greenish-gray legs and feet). Cattle Egret is rather short-legged for an egret, and less associated with aquatic habitats when feeding. They are commonly seen in fields, often near livestock, catching insects that they or the livestock disturb; there are even reports of them prodding resting cattle to get them moving so they will flush insects. Native to Africa, Cattle Egret arrived in South America in the late nineteenth century, established itself, and began expanding its range. First reports of its occurrence in the U.S. were in the 1940s, and it now breeds as far north as Michigan, Maine, and Ontario. Unlike many long-legged waders, it seems to thrive in the wake of man's alteration of the landscape. Postbreeding dispersal regularly takes it to areas far from its breeding range in late summer and fall. In the early 1980s several nests of Cattle Egrets were found on an island in Lake Barkley (Trigg County, Kentucky).

Green-backed Heron *Butorides striatus* 18¹/₂ in. **p.157**
Common summer (mid-March through Oct.) resident.
   This rather short-legged, solitary heron is the most common summer heron over most of LBL. In adults (see photograph) the upperparts are dark grayish-green (iridescent in good light), but appear black at a distance. The deep, blackish-green of the crown extends onto a jagged crest (not always visible) emerging from the upper nape. The face below the crown is dark chestnut, the chestnut extending down the sides of the neck and breast; the belly is light grayish. White on the upper throat extends as a line down the center of the lower throat, through the central breast, to the light belly. The bill is dark gray, and a white mustache line extends from the lower mandible back on each side of the face beneath the eye. Legs and feet are orange. Immature birds are similar, but have dull yellowish legs, are browner above, and have streaking instead of solid chestnut on the sides of the breast. Green-backed Heron frequents essentially all aquatic habitats of LBL, from lakeside to small, isolated ponds. One of several local names for this species is "fly-up-the-creek," descriptive of what it is likely to do when flushed along a stream. It nests singly or in small colonies, in brushy situations, sometimes at a surprising distance from water. The flushing call is a loud, coarse "skowp."

Black-crowned Night-Heron *Nycticorax nycticorax* 25 in.
Fairly common summer (April to mid-Oct.) resident.
   The night-herons are medium-sized, short-legged, heavy-bodied birds that feed by night and are rather inactive by

day. Adults of the two species of night-herons of LBL are easily distinguished; not so the immatures. Adult Black-crowned has a black crown and back, gray wings, and white underparts with a few long, unfrilled, white plumes extending back from the nape. The bill is black and stout, the legs and feet are yellow, yellow-green, or pinkish. The eyes are red and large, and there is a white forehead patch, and black lores. Immatures are dark brown above, coarsely spotted with white and buff. The underparts, head, and neck are buffy, streaked with brown. Full adult plumage is not attained until the birds are three years old. A breeding colony has existed for the past decade or so on a small island in Lake Barkley (Trigg County, Kentucky) and that vicinity is the best place to see them in LBL during the breeding season (but please don't disturb the rookery). After the young leave the nest the birds tend to disperse from the rookery site, but they remain rather clannish, and often assemble in groups at preferred day roosts, usually in trees. In flight they have powerful, steady wingbeats, and the feet barely extend beyond the tail. The call, often given at night or twilight, is a loud "kwark" or "kwok."

Yellow-crowned Night-Heron *Nyctanassa violacea* 25 in. Summer resident. Uncommon spring and summer (late March through July); rare fall (Aug. through Oct.).

This species is a bit slimmer than Black-crowned Night-Heron, with longer legs and a thinner neck. Adult plumage is all gray, except the head. The crown is white, cream, or buff, with short plumes extending from its hind margin during breeding season. The rest of the head is black, except for a white patch on the side of the face, below and behind the orange eye. The bill is stout and black, the legs and feet yellow. Immatures look very different from adults, and quite like immature Black-crowned Night-Herons. They are grayish-brown above (grayer than in Black-crowned), and freckled with more and smaller spots than in Black-crowned. The lower mandible of the bill of immatures is mostly dark, or just slightly paler at its base (in Black-crowneds, the lower mandible is paler than the upper for most of its length). In flight, the feet of Yellow-crowned Night-Heron extend well beyond the tail (not so in Black-crowned). Its call is similar to that of Black-crowned, but is higher pitched. It occurs in many wet habitats, but especially wooded swamps, and sometimes feeds during daylight. Less gregarious than Black-crowned, it may nest singly or in small colonies. In June 1966 I found two active nests of Yellow-crowned Night-Herons in an oak tree near a ridgetop on the well-manicured and much-visited grounds of Fort Donelson National Battlefield at Dover, Tennessee, just south of LBL.

Snow Goose *Chen caerulescens* 28 in.
Rare winter (Oct. through March) resident.

A solid white goose with black primaries seen in LBL is almost certain to be this species (though the extremely rare and distinctly smaller Ross' Goose is a very remote possibility). But many, probably most, Snow Geese seen in LBL are of the dark phase, with all slate-gray bodies (variously paler on the lower breast and belly), and white only on the head, upper neck, and upper and lower tail coverts. The two color phases were for years treated as separate species, the dark form known as "blue goose." The upper surfaces of the wings of the dark phase show black flight feathers, and are pearl-gray elsewhere. Bill, legs, and feet are pink. Black on the mandible margins makes the bird appear to have black lips. Immature white phase birds are mostly white below, but grayish atop the head and on the neck, back, and wing coverts. Immature dark phase birds are dusky all over, though lighter beneath, and have a white spot on the underside of the head just behind the mandible. Bills, legs, and feet of immatures of both color phases are dark. Some individuals, called "hybrids," are intermediate in appearance between the typical white and dark phases. Snow Geese are noisy, often crying in near-unison their yelp-like "uk-uk," or "hark-hark."

Canada Goose *Branta canadensis* 35 in. avg. (25-45 in. range) p.157
Permanent resident. Common winter (Oct. through April); fairly common summer.

The only breeding goose of LBL, this species exhibits an

exceptional range in size: some individuals are barely two feet long, while others may approach four feet. But except for size, they all look pretty much the same. They are brown above, paler brown beneath. The hindbelly, flanks, and undertail coverts are white; the rump and tail are black, separated by a white bar (the upper tail coverts). Bill, head, neck, legs, and feet are black, except for a broad white "chin strap." Canada Goose is primarily a vegetarian, and grazes on tender grasses (including young wheat), shoots, bulbs, berries, and grain, but it will also eat insects and other invertebrates when conveniently available. Remarkably successful restocking programs in recent decades have reestablished resident breeding populations in many parts of its former range, including LBL. Life-long pair bonds are common in this species, which normally doesn't breed until three years old. Potential lifespan is probably about 30 years, and a record exists of a wild bird that lived 23 years; life expectancy of wild birds, however, is much less than these figures. The long, symmetrical lines or "V" formations of Canada Geese in flight are an impressive and familiar sight. Commonly called "honkers," their call varies with the size of the goose, but, for larger birds at least, is a honk-like "ga-ronk" or "honk-ga-ronk."

Wood Duck *Aix sponsa* 18¹/₂ in.   **p.158**
Permanent resident. Fairly common summer (March through Oct.); uncommon winter.

The breeding male (see photograph) is resplendent to the point of gaudiness, and is not likely to be confused with any other species in LBL. The plumage pattern is too complex to describe here (see photograph). The female, by comparison, is quite drab. She is dark above, paler and speckled below, and has a gray, crested head, with a white patch surrounding each eye. Wood Ducks often perch in trees, and nest in tree cavities. The nest cavity, commonly a natural cavity or old woodpecker hole, is typically 5 to 40 feet high, and either over water or within 600 feet of the nearest water. The hatchlings have sharp toenails which they use to climb the walls of the nest cavity to the entrance hole, where they may peer out for a while and then

28

fearlessly launch themselves into the air. With tiny, fuzzy wings and webbed feet fully extended, they do their best to slow their free fall. Their fluffy coat of down helps to absorb the energy at impact. Often they bounce when they hit the ground (of course, if the nest is over water they splash), right themselves, and walk straight to the nearest water, where mother is usually waiting. Nest boxes erected in wooded swamps have done much in helping bring this species back from very low population sizes just a few decades ago. Wood Duck eats seeds, acorns, grain, and invertebrates. Its call includes a distinctive "whoa-eeek," and a high, thin, lisping "jeeee."

Green-winged Teal *Anas crecca* 14 in.
Winter resident. Fairly common spring (March to late May) and fall (Aug. through Nov.); uncommon winter.

The smallest dabbling duck in LBL. Its darting flight a rapid wing beat make it appear to be a fast flier. The breeding male is mostly gray above, with a speckled, buff-colored breast, a chestnut head and neck, and a broad green stripe extending from before the eye, back across the face, and onto the neck; the belly is light. The wings above are dark, and the speculum is iridescent green. On the water a white crescent shows on each side before the wing, and a buff rump patch may be visible. The female is mottled grayish-brown above, lighter beneath, with a whitish belly and a buff-colored patch beneath the tail. Green-winged Teal is usually seen in shallow water situations, especially marshes, ponds, and flooded fields. The call of males is one to several short, clear whistles; females sort of quack. The diet is varied, and includes both plant and animal material.

American Black Duck *Anas rubripes* 23 in.
Fairly common winter (Sept. to mid-May) resident.

This close relative of the Mallard (the two species hybridize readily in certain parts of their ranges) is charcoal gray over most of its body, with a brown head and neck. The speculum is violet or purplish, with a black border (very narrow whitish border present on trailing edge, i.e. at the extreme tips of secondaries). Legs and feet are orange to reddish-orange, brighter in male than in female. The bill is yellow in adult males, a duller yellow mottled with black in adult females, and greenish in immatures. American Black Ducks resemble female Mallards but are darker (hence they are sometimes called "black mallards") and lack a conspicuous white border to the speculum. In flight, when seen from below, all plumages show a sharp contrast between the white wing linings and the dark body and flight feathers. The call is a "quack," indistinguishable from that of Mallard.

Mallard *Anas platyrhynchos* 24 in. p.158
Permanent resident. Common winter (Sept. to mid-May); uncommon summer.

The adult male (see photograph) of this dabbling duck species, often called "greenhead" by hunters, is unmistakable with its brilliant, metallic-green head and neck, bright yellow bill, white collar at base of the neck, and chestnut breast. The back is basically gray (but not evenly so), and the sides are a lighter gray. The tail is whitish, set off by black upper- and undertail coverts. The speculum is blue, with white borders; legs and feet are orange. In flight, males overhead show a dark breast, a white neck ring, and a light belly and tail separated by the black undertail coverts. Females look very different, more like American Black Duck than like male Mallards. They have orange bills mottled with dark brown, and are mottled brown over most of their bodies (but lighter than American Black Duck). Mallards are the mainstay of duck hunters in the region, and over much of North America. Historic changes in their breeding range have brought them into increased competition with American Black Duck, which has similar habits, and Mallard seems to be doing well in that contest. The call of Mallard is a loud "quack," among several other sounds.

Northern Pintail *Anas acuta* 25 in. p.159
Uncommon winter (Sept. to mid-May) resident.

A large dabbler, the adult male (on left in photograph) is

an elegant bird with his long, slender neck, attractive but subdued colors, and sprig-like tail. The body is gray above and on the sides; underparts are white, except for black undertail coverts. White on the breast is continued two-thirds of the way up the front of the neck, with a narrow white stripe extending on each side up to the back of the head. The head, upper neck, and nape are rich, chocolate brown; the bill is small and bluish-black. A black, elongated patch is usually visible on the midside of the body when the bird is not flying, and there is a buff or white patch aside the rump in front of the black undertail coverts. The wings above are bluish-gray, with a green speculum bordered in front by a buff line and in back by a white one. The long, needle-like central tail feathers are black, the others gray. Legs and feet are gray. Females (on right in photograph) are mostly mottled brown, with a brown speculum; their tails, though pointed, lack the very long central feathers of the male. Females quack, and males give a double-noted, piping whistle. The diet is mostly plant material, but includes some aquatic animals (small fish, tadpoles, and invertebrates).

Blue-winged Teal *Anas discors* 15½ in.
Common spring (late Feb. through May) and fall (Aug. through Oct.) transient.

A small dabbler, fond of ponds, marshes, and sloughs. The breeding male has a dark gray or blue-gray head and upper neck, with a large white crescent on each side of the face before the eye. The lower neck, breast, sides, and belly are tan, finely speckled with blackish spots. The front half of the inner wing is powder blue, and some of this may show in the grounded bird as a horizontal blue line along the side (or it may be covered by body feathers). The flanks show a small white spot, just in front of the black rump. The bill is black, the legs and feet yellow. The green speculum may have a partial white border in front. Females are mostly mottled brown everywhere, lighter on the head, upper neck, and belly. They have the blue wing patch, however, and usually a light spot on the lores. The call of the male is a high-pitched series of peep notes; the female quacks faintly. Blue-winged Teal is one of the earliest migrant ducks to arrive in LBL in the fall, and, on average, one of the latest to pass through in the spring. In some areas an early teal hunting season is established to allow hunters to take advantage of their early fall migration.

Northern Shoveler *Anas clypeata* 19 in.
Winter resident. Uncommon fall (Sept. through Nov.) and spring (mid-Feb. to mid-May); rare winter.

A medium-sized duck with a "spoon bill" (in fact, "spoon-bill" is one of its common names). Adult males have a glossy green head and neck, white breast, and rufous sides and belly. The flanks are white, and the tail black, except for its white outer feathers. The back is brown down its center, with a white streak along each side above the wing. The wings above look very much like those of Blue-winged Teal, with a green speculum separated by a white border from the powder blue forewing patch. The bill is unusually long and wide, but not very deep (i.e., like a shovel). Legs and feet are orange, and the bill is black. Female plumage is like that of female Blue-winged Teal, but the larger size and distinctive bill of Northern Shoveler make distinguishing between the two fairly easy. The female's bill is orange at its margins, brown otherwise. Immature males may have a light crescent on their face, suggestive of adult male Blue-winged Teal. Males are mostly silent; females utter a soft "quack." Northern Shoveler is a filter feeder, straining small (even planktonic) plants and animals from the surface and near-surface waters of ponds, marshes, sloughs, and mudflat edges through comblike plates along the inner edge of its bill.

Gadwall *Anas strepera* 20 in.
Winter resident. Uncommon fall (Sept. through Nov.) and spring (March to mid-May), fairly common winter.

A sleek, medium-sized, rather drab duck, but still attractive. The adult male has a grayish body (actually it is finely barred black and white) with a black rump. The belly is whitish; the head and neck are brown, often lighter on the lower half of the face. The bill is black, and the legs and feet are orange. Several long, rusty-edged back feathers are usually not discernible in the field. The upper wing surface is unique among the dabbling ducks of LBL in having, in all plumages, a white speculum, bordered on the front and outside edge by black. Females are dusky, mottled brown over all of the body (except for the whitish belly), and have a gray bill bordered with orange. Calls include a weak quack given by the female, and various clucks and whistles from the male. Though a dabbling duck, capable of springing directly from the water's surface into the air without a takeoff run, it can dive (actually most dabblers can—but seldom do), and sometimes does in search of insects, mollusks, or small vertebrates. Most of its winter diet, however, is plant material.

American Wigeon *Anas americana* 21 in.

Winter resident. Uncommon fall (mid-Sept. through Nov.) and spring (March to mid-May); fairly common winter.

Formerly called "baldpate," this medium-sized dabbler is bald on its pate (top of head) only in the sense that Bald Eagle is bald—its head is covered with white feathers. The male is white on the forehead and crown, and a broad, glossy green stripe extends from before the eye back across the face and down the neck. The front and lower face and the neck are gray. The body is mostly pinkish-brown, darker above than below, with a white belly and flanks. The undertail coverts are black. The bill is pale, bluish-gray with a black tip, and the legs and feet are gray. From above the wings show a green speculum and a large white forewing patch. Females are mostly mottled brown with a grayish head; they lack the white forehead, crown, and forewing patch. The call of males is a three-note whistle, the middle note higher pitched: "whew-whee-whew." The female quacks. American Wigeon feeds mostly on leaves, buds, bulbs, etc., of aquatic vegetation, as well as on various aquatic invertebrates. It will also come ashore to graze, or feed on grains.

Canvasback *Aythya valisineria* 21 in.

Winter resident. Rare fall (late Oct. through Nov.) and spring (March through April); uncommon winter.

A large diving duck, with a distinctive head profile. Males are very light gray above, whitish on the sides and belly. The breast, tail, and tail coverts are black, and contrast sharply with the light-colored central portions of the bird. Head and neck are chestnut, blending into a blackish crown and forehead. The long, black bill is deep at its base, and the junction of it with the sloping forehead gives a flattish profile that is distinctive, and one of the best field characters in all plumages. The eye is ruby red. The wings above are gray, with darker primaries. Females are mostly light brown, reddish on the head, neck, and breast, and have dark eyes. Strong, fast fliers, Canvasbacks often form straight or V-shaped lines aloft. They prefer open, but not necessarily deep, waters, where they dive for aquatic vegetation and invertebrates, including small mussels. Though usually silent off the breeding grounds, the male can coo and the female can quack.

Redhead *Aythya americana* 20 in. **p.159**

Uncommon winter (mid-Oct. through April) resident.

Similar to Canvasback, the "roundhead Redhead" lacks the distinctive, sloping head profile of that species (see account of Canvasback for basic description), and is a bit smaller. The body of the male Redhead (on right in photograph) is a medium gray, noticeably darker than in Canvasback. Eyes are yellow, and the blue bill has a black tip and whitish subterminal ring. Darker than the female Canvasback, the female Redhead (on left in photograph) is basically all brown (except for a whitish belly), has the rounded head shape characteristic of her species, a pale area on the lower front of her face, and a dark eye. Males may meow and purr during courtship, but females are usually silent. Redhead feeds extensively on aquatic plants, but also eats aquatic invertebrates. More likely to be found on shallow pools and marshes than Canvasback, but also seen on deep, open waters, sometimes in large rafts.

Ring-necked Duck *Aythya collaris* 16½ in.   **p.160**
Common winter (mid-Oct. through April) resident.

This smallish diver is more likely to be seen on ponds, marshes, and even wooded swamps than are the other diving ducks, though it also frequents large, open bodies of water. The male (see photograph) has a black head and neck (purple in good light), breast, back, and rump. The sides are gray, and a vertical white patch in front of the gray side (which extends upward slightly in front of the folded wing) is a good field mark at surprising distances. The bill is gray on its basal two-thirds, with a white ring beyond that, and a black tip. The face has a narrow ring of white feathers encircling the base of the bill. The back of the crown often has a peaked appearance. The namesake feature of this species, a brown ring at the base of the neck, is useless as a field character because you can never see it. The female is dark, dusky brown, with a light eyering, a pale face, and a bill patterned as in the male but less vividly colored. From above, the extended wings show a broad gray area along the trailing edge, lightest near the body and darkest on the primaries. The diet is mostly plant material, but aquatic invertebrates are taken when convenient. Males may whistle, females purr or snarl.

Greater Scaup *Aythya marila* 17½ in.
Extremely rare winter (Nov. through Feb.) resident.

See account of Lesser Scaup for a basic description of this species, as the two are nearly identical. Greater Scaup is primarily a duck of marine coastal areas and the Great Lakes region, and few make it to LBL. Look for it mingling in flocks of Lesser Scaup, where you can compare the two species. The head of Greater Scaup normally looks black, but under the right lighting conditions (sun to your back) the head may glisten with a green sheen; Lesser Scaup shows a purple—only occasionally green—sheen. A better distinguishing character is the head in profile: smoothly round over the top and back, rather than "pointy" as in Lesser Scaup. The flanks of Greater Scaup tend to be whiter but—depending on the season, probably the age of the bird, and possibly the genetic makeup of the individuals involved—there may be overlap between the two species in this character. Probably the best field character (though it can only be used for birds in flight and even then requires a good look) is the whitish stripe on the trailing edge of the upper wing surface; in Lesser Scaup the stripe is restricted to the secondaries, while in Greater it extends on toward the wing tip, through at least half of the primaries (though only the outer half, or vane, of each primary is actually white). Trying to distinguish between these two species is tough, but with a good scope, warm clothing, a prefrontal lobotomy, and the sun to your back it can be a pleasant way to spend a winter afternoon. Greater Scaup is omnivorous. It's usually silent except when courting.

Lesser Scaup *Aythya affinis* 16½ in.   p.160
Common winter (Oct. through April) resident.

The male (see photograph) has a gray (actually finely barred black and white) back, light gray sides, and white lower sides and belly. Head and neck are black (sometimes purplish, or purplish/greenish, in good light), as are the breast, upper and lower tail coverts, and tail. The blue-gray bill ("bluebill" is a common hunter's name for this species) has a black "nail" at its extreme tip. The eyes are yellow. The upper surface of the wing is mostly dark, with a broad, white stripe on the trailing edge of the inner wing (i.e., on the secondaries). The back of the head is angular in profile, but not as much as in Ring-necked Duck. Female is mostly brown (excepting the white abdomen), with a white face patch at the base of the bill (much more distinct than in female Ring-necked Duck). For tips on distinguishing this species from the very similar Greater Scaup (which is extremely rare in LBL), see account of that species. One of the most common diving ducks of LBL waters, Lesser Scaup is usually seen on the larger lakes, often near shore. Its feeding habits are omnivorous. This species is normally silent on its wintering grounds, but it can quack and whistle.

36

Common Goldeneye *Bucephala clangula* 18½ in. **p.161**
Winter resident. Uncommon fall (Nov.) and spring (March through April); fairly common winter.

A medium-sized, compact, stubby-billed diving duck, with a big head. Adult males (see photograph) have a glossy, dark green head (usually looks black in the field), with a large, round, white spot on each side of the face below and before the golden eye. The neck, breast, sides, and belly are white, contrasting with the black back and rump. The wing's upper surface is dark except for a large white patch occupying all but the leading edge of the inner wing, and in flight this patch serves as a good field character. The tail is dark, the legs and feet are orange to yellowish. Female has a solid brown head, a white collar on the upper neck, grayish lower neck, back, and sides, and white breast and belly. Courting males may whistle loudly. In flight, the wings produce a distinctive whistling sound, the basis for the hunter's name of "whistler" for this species. Common Goldeneyes prefer large expanses of open water where, when feeding, they seem to spend as much time beneath the surface as on it. They eat fish, crustaceans, insects, and some plant material.

Bufflehead *Bucephala albeola* 14 in. **p.161**
Winter resident. Uncommon fall (Nov.) and spring (March through April); fairly common winter.

One of our smallest ducks (about pigeon size). It's difficult to look at Bufflehead and not think "chunky"; the word "butterball" serves as a common name for it to many people. Males (see photograph) have black heads, with a distinct green or purple sheen, and a large, triangular white patch extending from each eye to completely encircle the back of the head. The white neck may be hidden when the bird's head is retracted. Breast, belly, sides, and flanks are also white; the back is black. The bill is short and dark gray, the eyes black, the legs and feet orange. Nearly the entire inner wing is white above, visible in flight. The female has a gray-brown body (darker above), and brown head with a large white patch on each side of the face below and behind the eye. The upper surface of her wing has a small white patch on the trailing edge, next to the body. The call of the male is a squeaky whistle; females may give a subdued quack. Diet includes more animal than plant matter, but some seeds are eaten. Bufflehead is rather approachable for a duck, and easily decoyed by hunters. It prefers open water to ponds and marshes.

Hooded Merganser *Lophodytes cucullatus* 17½ in. **p.162**
Permanent resident. Fairly common fall and winter (Oct. through Feb.); uncommon spring (March to mid-May); rare summer.

Hooded Merganser gets my vote for the most elegantly attired bird of LBL. The displaying breeding male (see photograph) is gorgeous. Smallest of the three species of mergansers, or "fish ducks," in LBL, it has the thin, hook-tipped bill with saw-tooth-edged mandibles characteristic of the group. The bill is adapted for catching and holding small fish (its dietary staple) and frogs, tadpoles, insects, and crustaceans. Males have black heads, with an erectile white-with-black-border crest, a black bill, and yellow eyes. The neck, back, and tail are black; the breast and belly are white, with two black bars extending down from the back onto each side of the breast. Sides, flanks, and undertail coverts are russet. The inner half of the upper wing surface has a gray patch up front and a white patch on the secondaries. The female is blackish on the back, brown on the sides, and gray on the breast. Her crest is russet instead of white and black, and she has darker eyes than the male. Hooded Merganser prefers protected bays of the larger lakes, and even wooded swamps. This species breaks the rule that ducks proficient at diving and underwater swimming must "taxi" along the water's surface in order to become airborne; it can "jump" (using both wings and feet) directly into the air. The male gives croaking or grunting noises.

Common Merganser *Mergus merganser* 25 in. **p.162**
Winter resident. Uncommon fall (late Oct. through Nov.); fairly common winter and spring (Dec. through March).

Adult male (see photograph) has a black (dark, irides-cent green in good light and up close), head and upper neck. The back has a black center bordered on each side by a broad, white stripe. The lower neck, breast, sides, flanks, belly, and undertail coverts are white. The lower back of the head may show just a suggestion of a crest. The rump, uppertail coverts, and tail are gray. The reddish-orange bill is long and thin, with a sharply hooked black tip. The legs and feet are reddish-orange, and the eyes are dark. The upper surface of the inner wing is mostly white on its inner half, and the outer half is black. Females have brown heads and upper necks, with a white upper throat and a jagged crest at the lower back of the head. Otherwise females are gray—very light gray on the lower neck and breast. The line separating the brown upper throat from the light gray lower throat is quite sharp, and is the best field character for distinguishing this female from the female Red-breasted Merganser. White on the upper wing surface is restricted to the speculum in females. Diet consists mostly of fish. This species rarely vocalizes.

Red-breasted Merganser *Mergus serrator* 23 in.
Winter resident. Uncommon fall (Oct. through Nov.) and spring (March to mid-May); rare winter.

The adult male Red-breasted Merganser looks like Common Merganser, but is a bit smaller, has a distinct crest (often appears doubled, i.e. with a notch in its trailing edge), a red eye, gray sides and flanks, and a brown breast streaked or spotted with black. The white lower neck appears as a white collar when the neck is retracted. Females similar to female Common Mergansers, but differ in that the light-colored breast and lower throat blend gradually into the brown of the upper throat. The numerous tooth-like serrations of the mandibles, used in catching fish, are the basis of the name of "sawbill" for this species and Common Merganser (true teeth in the mouth of a merganser—or of any living species of bird—are of course as scarce as hen's teeth). The flight of mergansers is strong, often low over the water, the birds in a flock tending to line up single file. Their long, narrow bills are held straight out in front of the fully extended neck, in the same plane as the body, giving them a distinctive profile. Red-breasted Mergansers are usually silent.

Ruddy Duck *Oxyura jamaicensis* 15½ in.
Rare winter (Oct. through April) resident.

A small, stocky, big-headed duck whose habit of holding its spiny tail cocked up suggests a giant wren sitting on the water. (Ruddy Duck belongs to a group of ducks known as "stifftails.") The breeding plumage of the males—often not acquired until springtime, after they have departed LBL—is all ruddy except for a black head and tail, and white belly. The front two-thirds of the face below the eye is white. The bill is a brilliant powder blue, looking as though some overenthusiastic taxidermist had been at work on it with model airplane paint. The winter male is brown instead of ruddy, and has a dark brown (instead of black) head. The face patch is dingy white, and the bill is gray or blue-gray. Females look like winter males, but have a dark horizontal line through the light cheek patch. In all plumages the wings are solid dark gray above. Ruddy Duck is commonly seen by itself, or with other Ruddys. They often dive to escape danger rather than fly, or they may simply swim away when approached. Diet is mostly aquatic invertebrates, but some plant material is eaten. On their wintering grounds they occur most commonly on larger bodies of water. Ruddy Duck is just one of several species of waterfowl that may practice brood parasitism, laying eggs in the unguarded nests of other species of ducks or of other Ruddys. Silent when in LBL.

Black Vulture *Coragyps atratus* 25 in.
Uncommon permanent resident.

The smaller of the two vultures (or "buzzards," as they are locally known) of LBL, Black Vulture is a valuable member of the local scavenger's club. Its plumage is all black, except for conspicuous white patches near the wing tips, at the base of the primaries. The head, legs, and feet are naked and gray. The tail is short, the retracted feet in flight reaching approximately to its tip. An accomplished soarer, Black Vulture is most often seen as it circles overhead, often with other vultures, riding updrafts. Black Vulture may be distinguished from Turkey Vulture by the former's white wing patches; its stubbier, more fan-shaped tail; its habit of giving several rapid wing beats and then gliding;

and its flat profile in soaring flight (the wings being held in a plane extending from the bird's body, rather than in a shallow "V"). Vultures, as carrion feeders, have excellent vision, moderately hooked beaks (by raptor standards), and weak talons. The naked head is their way of avoiding soiled head feathers as they probe deep within a carcass during feeding. Though primarily carrion feeders, Black Vultures have predaceous tendencies and sometimes take live small vertebrates, or attack larger ones that are sick but not dead yet. Vultures are mute. They usually nest in a large, hollow tree, stump, or log, beneath the floor or in the loft of an outbuilding or abandoned house, or on a cliff ledge.

Turkey Vulture *Cathartes aura* 28 in. p.163
Fairly common permanent resident.

A large, eagle-like bird (wingspan up to six feet—not quite eagle size), its conspicuousness (because of its large size and habit of soaring) belies its real abundance. As it soars it sniffs the air and scans the terrain below for carrion. (The keen sense of smell that Turkey Vultures have been demonstrated to possess is quite unusual among birds, most of whom rely primarily on their senses of vision and hearing.) The plumage of Turkey Vulture is brownish-black. The extended wings lack the white primary patches of Black Vulture, but have a two-toned appearance (as seen from below) because of the contrast between the lighter-colored flight feathers and the darker wing linings. The pink, naked, wrinkled head of the adult (see photograph) is strikingly grotesque; black "shadows" under the eyes, a prominent white tip on the moderately hooked beak, and a hunchbacked appearance while perched or walking all add to the effect. ("Ugly as homemade sin," according to one observer.) But they are transformed by flight into graceful, floating creatures, seldom needing to exert themselves by flapping their wings, gliding along on updrafts, their wings held outstretched and motionless in a shallow "V." The pink legs and feet (immatures have blackish heads, legs, and feet) are rather weak, and not used for transporting or dismembering objects as is common in hawks and eagles. Food is carried to the nest—usually in a natural cavity or on a ledge—in the crop, and regurgitated for the nestlings. The downy, white young are appealing, but if disturbed attempt to discourage predators by explosively vomiting their most recent meal of semidigested, putrified meat—deterring all but the most determined.

Osprey *Pandion haliaetus* 23 in.   **p.163**
Uncommon spring (mid-March to mid-May) and fall (Sept. through Oct.) transient; rare summer resident.

The "fish hawk"—an apt name for this species—is about the size of Red-tailed Hawk, noticeably smaller than an eagle. The upperparts are chocolate brown, the tail is banded gray and brown. The underparts and head are predominantly white, except for blackish patches at the wrists (a good field mark—see photograph), a dark brown stripe from the eye to the neck, dark tips on the primaries, and a dark band near the tip of the tail (adult females also have scattered spots in a band across the breast). Immatures have buff-colored edges to the feathers above, giving them a somewhat speckled appearance. The talons are extremely long and sharp. Osprey is the only raptor in LBL that plunges, feet first, into the water after fish. (Eagles may use their talons to snatch fish from the water, but must swim—with laborious wing beats—to shore if they become immersed.) Decimated by DDT in the environment during the 1950s and 60s, Osprey is recovering in most parts of its range since that chemical was banned from widespread use in this country in 1972. Aloft, the wings of Osprey appear to bend slightly down (an inverted "V" effect) and back (a swept-wing effect) at the wrist. It often hovers or perches over water as it watches for live fish below, which are almost its only food. A bulky nest of sticks is placed near the top of a tall tree, on electrical transmission line towers, or on specially provided nesting platforms. Osprey's call is a short series of loud, emphatic, whistled notes.

Bald Eagle *Haliaeetus leucocephalus* 36 in.   **p.164**
Permanent resident. Uncommon winter (Oct. through March); rare summer.

The largest raptor of LBL, the unmistakable adults (see photograph) are dark brown everywhere except the solid white tail, head, and neck. The bill, legs, and feet are bright yellow. Four or five years are normally required before adult plumage is attained, and the immatures, lacking the white head and tail, resemble adult Golden Eagles. Immature Bald Eagles may be distinguished from adult Golden Eagles by the appearance of the lower surfaces of the wings; immature Bald Eagle has light wing linings contrasting with darker flight feathers, whereas adult Golden Eagle shows no such contrast (in fact, the wing linings are likely to be slightly darker than the flight feathers). In soaring flight, eagles have a flat-winged profile, rather than the shallow "V" of Turkey Vulture or the bowed and swept-back look of Osprey. The banning of DDT and the education of gunners have saved this species in the lower 48 states, and beginning in 1983, several successful nestings of Bald Eagles have occurred in and around LBL. Bald Eagle feeds mostly on fish, often dead or enfeebled, which it may scavenge on the beaches, snatch from the water, or pirate in mid-air from Osprey; it will also take waterfowl (especially the sick or wounded), small mammals, and carrion. Hacking programs, designed to re-establish breeding populations, have played a significant role in the recent and ongoing recovery of this species in the lower 48 states. The voice of Bald Eagle is less of a scream than a cackle (or, screaming cackle, if you like).

Northern Harrier *Circus cyaneus* male 17 in./female 19 in.
                                                                p.164
Rare winter (Sept. through April) resident.

The adult male (bird at top in photograph is a male molting into his adult plumage) is a beautiful, sleek bird. It is light gray above, with black wing tips, a white rump, and a dark band near the tip of the long tail. Underneath, it is gray on the throat and breast, mostly whitish elsewhere, and speckled with reddish spots or bars. The legs are long and yellow. Adult females (bird at bottom in photograph) are similar but deep brown instead of light gray above, and with buffier underparts more heavily spotted and streaked with brown. Immatures resemble females, but show much cinnamon, especially below. A hawk of open, grassy fields and marshes, it "harries" small mammals (its primary diet) by flying low and slow over the ground, listening and watching for scurrying prey, which are pounced upon when detected. Northern Harrier may fly over 100 miles in a day as it systematically searches the countryside. Its flight is easy, with intermittent episodes of flapping and gliding, the wings held slightly up in a shallow "V" when gliding. During migration Northern Harriers may be seen at considerable altitudes. They do not vocalize, except at their nests.

Sharp-shinned Hawk *Accipiter striatus* male 10½ in./ female 12½ in. **p.165**
Permanent resident. Uncommon winter (mid-Sept. to mid-May) and rare summer.
The smaller of the two species of accipiters, or "bird hawks" (called that because small birds are their dietary staple), to be expected in LBL. As an accipiter, Sharp-shinned Hawk has short, rounded wings (adapted to maneuvering in dense vegetation, where its prey commonly seeks refuge), and a rather long, parallel-sided tail. The sexes are similar in appearance, but females are distinctly larger than males, weighing up to half-again as much. Adults (see photograph) have slate gray upperparts, and white underparts heavily barred with rufous. The tail has four straight, dark bands across it, and when not spread is either square or slightly notched across its tip. The legs are long, and the feet are yellow. The fiery-red eyes of adults are striking. Immatures are brown above, white streaked with brown below, and have yellow or yellowish-orange eyes. The characteristic flight of accipiters is a series of powerful, rapid wing beats, followed by a short glide, then repeating this sequence. They sometimes soar, especially during courtship and migration. Male Sharp-shinneds, because of their small size, are relatively easy to distinguish from Cooper's Hawks, but female Sharp-shinneds may be nearly as large as some male Cooper's, making field identification very difficult. Probably the shape of the tail tip is

the single most useful field character in such cases, but a good look is required, and often all one can do is call the bird an accipiter. The call, not often heard except near the nest, is a long series of "kiks," higher pitched than Cooper's.

Cooper's Hawk *Accipiter cooperii* male 15¹/₂ in./female 18 in.
Uncommon permanent resident.

The larger of LBL's two regular accipiters. Nearly identical in appearance to Sharp-shinned Hawk, except for size (though female Sharp-shinneds may be nearly as large as male Cooper's) and shape of the tip of the folded tail (see account of Sharp-shinned Hawk for description of appearance, and tips on how to distinguish these two species). Sometimes called the "blue darter" because of the blue-gray upperparts of the adults and their habit of darting into the woods as they seek refuge or pursue prey. Though Cooper's Hawks prey mostly on small to medium-sized birds, they also take significantly more small mammals than do Sharp-shinned Hawks. Like Sharp-shinned Hawks, they may take advantage of the concentrations of birds attracted to backyard bird feeders. Another on the list of DDT victims, populations of Cooper's Hawk seem to be recovering somewhat. The nest is commonly in a conifer, sometimes in a deciduous tree; they may use old nests of other species, such as crows. The call, usually in defense of its nest, is a long series (15-20) of "kahs."

Red-shouldered Hawk *Buteo lineatus* 18 in.   **p.165**
Uncommon permanent resident.

Of the three species of buteo hawks commonly seen in LBL, this one is intermediate in size (smaller than Red-tailed, larger than Broad-winged). The buteos (or "buzzard hawks") are rather plump-bodied, short-winged, and fan-tailed compared to other groups of hawks. They are accomplished soarers, and are often seen high overhead as they drift lazily along. Buteos are notoriously varied in their appearance, and you should consult a good field guide (see list in back of this book) for details on that variation.

Typical adult Red-shouldered Hawks (see photograph) in LBL are brown above, mottled with buff on the back and white on the wings, with reddish patches (sometimes barely noticeable) on the shoulders. The underparts are barred rufous and white. The tail has wide black bands alternating with narrow white bands, visible both from above and below. All plumages are likely to show white patches or "windows" at the base of the primaries when viewed from below. Immatures are mostly brown above, white-streaked-with-brown below, and have finely barred brown and black (rather than white and black) tails. They prefer dense woodlands, especially near water. Their short, loud "kee-aarrr" call (second note lower pitched) is often imitated by Blue Jay.

Broad-winged Hawk *Buteo platypterus* 16 in. **p.166**
Uncommon summer (late March to mid-Oct.) resident.

Our smallest buteo in LBL (see account of Red-shouldered Hawk for a characterization of the group), about the size of American Crow. A woodland species, but less associated with moist situations than is Red-shouldered Hawk. The adult Broad-winged Hawk (see photograph) is dark brown above, with white underparts heavily barred with brown or rufous. The wings underneath are quite light, but edged with black. Black and white bands on the tail are of approximately equal width, and broader and fewer than in Red-shouldered Hawk. Immatures are light on the breast and belly, with brown streaks (rather than bars, as in adults). The banding pattern on the immature's tail is finer and less vivid than in the adult, similar to that of an immature Red-shouldered Hawk. It feeds on a wide variety of small vertebrates, including nestling birds (it is not agile enough to catch many adult birds). Flocks of Broad-winged Hawks, sometimes mixed with other species, may be seen during migration—especially in the fall. The call is a high-pitched, two-syllabled scream, or whistle, the second syllable extended and fading.

Red-tailed Hawk *Buteo jamaicensis* 22 in. **p.166**
Fairly common permanent resident.

One of the most widespread hawks in North America, occurring over all of the lower 48 states of the U.S., all of Mexico, most of Canada, and parts of Alaska. It is quite variable in appearance not only over its vast range, but even at a particular locality. The largest regular hawk of LBL (the extremely rare Rough-legged Hawk is as large), and the most abundant as well, at all seasons. A typical buteo in shape and flight silhouette (see account of Red-shouldered Hawk for a characterization of buteo hawks), adults (see photograph) are usually easily recognized by the rufous upper surface of the fan-shaped tail. The upperparts otherwise are brown, mottled with buff or gray. The underparts are mostly light, but a band of dark streaks—or "bellyband"—is usually present, contrasting with the white of the breast. The tail viewed from below is light, showing no conspicuous banding; when backlighted, the rufous of the upper surface may show through the tail, making it appear pinkish. Immatures have a finely barred, brown and gray tail, but otherwise resemble adults. Red-tailed Hawk is often seen as it soars overhead, or perches conspicuously atop a fence post, utility pole, or dead tree, especially along roadsides and habitat edges. It prefers to hunt in open or semiopen areas rather than in dense woodlands. Diet is mostly small mammals, but will take birds, snakes, lizards, and frogs. Its call is a loud, piercing scream, beginning explosively, and then falling gradually in both pitch and volume.

Rough-legged Hawk *Buteo lagopus* 22 in.
Extremely rare winter (Oct. through March) resident.

As large as Red-tailed Hawk, but with a distinctive tail; the tail is long, and basically white to pale buff, with one or a few dark bands. Two phases—a light and a dark—occur. Consult a standard field guide (several are listed at the end of this book) for descriptions of the considerable variation that exists among the different phases, ages, and sexes. Adapted to nesting on the treeless tundra of extreme northern Canada and Alaska, it prefers open country even on its wintering grounds. There it perches or hovers as it scans for small mammals. It is our only buteo to regularly hover, though other local species may do so occasionally. Our only hawk with legs feathered to the base of the toes (though Golden Eagle also has that trait). Silent in LBL.

Golden Eagle *Aquila chrysaetos* 35 in.
Rare winter (Nov. through Feb.) resident.

About the size of Bald Eagle, Golden Eagle is less associated with bodies of water over most of its range. It is also less of a scavenger and more of an active predator (especially on medium-sized mammals), though it will feed on carrion when live prey is scarce. The adult is mostly dark brown, with obscure gray bands on the tail. At close range, a golden-brown wash may be visible on the hind neck and back of the head. The bill is grayish-brown to black. Immatures are easily identified by the white patches at the primary bases and their white tails with broad, dark terminal bands. (See account of Bald Eagle for more information on how to distinguish these two species.) Golden Eagle rarely vocalizes during the non-breeding season, but it can utter bark-like yelps, either singly or as a series.

American Kestrel *Falco sparverius* male 9 in./female 10 in. **p.167**
Uncommon permanent resident.

The smallest hawk of LBL, about the size of American Robin. Surprisingly scarce in LBL, considering the availability of extensive, apparently suitable habitat and how common it is in adjacent areas. American Kestrel is a falcon—a group of speedy hawks with longish, parallel-sided tails, and long, narrow, pointed wings. Peregrine Falcon and Merlin are two other falcons that occur rarely in the region, but neither is a regular in LBL. The adult male American Kestrel (see photograph) is a beautiful bird with a black-barred rufous back, and a rufous tail tipped by a black band (actually there is a narrow white margin at the extreme tip of the tail, but it is not usually evident in the field). The wings are a striking bluish-gray, blackish toward the primary tips. The underparts are cinnamon buff on the breast, fading to buff on the belly, with scattered black spots, especially on the sides and flanks. The handsome and colorful head has a rufous crown patch surrounded by a blue corona, a white face and throat, two short, vertical black bars aside the face, and a buff nape bearing a black "eyespot" in its center. Females are similar, but with rusty wings, finely barred tail, and more streaking below. Immatures are like adults, but with more spotting. Commonly perches on utility wires and fences as it watches for prey (mostly insects and mice, but also lizards, small snakes, and small birds). It often hovers. A hole or cranny nester, it uses woodpecker holes, bird boxes, and eaves of buildings as nest sites. The call is a short series of high, shrill notes: "k-lee, k-lee, k-lee, k-lee, k-lee."

Wild Turkey *Meleagris gallopavo* male 48 in./female 36 in. **p.167**
Fairly common permanent resident.

A very large bird, adult males are nearly four feet from tip of bill to tip of tail. Land Between The Lakes is a stronghold of this species in the region; it apparently was never extirpated from those parts of northern LBL that made up the Hillman Land Company holdings and later the Kentucky Woodlands National Wildlife Refuge (established in 1938). Wild Turkey looks like its derivative, the barnyard turkey, but has chestnut on the tips of the tail feathers rather than white. The beautifully ugly head of breeding males (see photograph) is blue and red, naked, wrinkled, and wattled, looking as though it may just have emerged from a mangling by the jaws of some large predator. Powerful fliers for short distances, they prefer to flee by running instead. Quite social birds, males are larger than females, more splendidly colored, and have spurred legs and usually a larger "beard" (a tuft of hairlike feathers, sometimes several inches long, protruding from the breast). Breeding males maintain a harem of several hens which they "gobble" together with their distinctive, loud, gobbling call. Though Wild Turkeys roost in trees, they forage for food on the ground, in or near woodlands. They eat various seeds—including many acorns—and insects. Though wary and difficult to approach, they may be lured into gun range by a hidden hunter imitating the call. Over-hunting and introduced poultry diseases eliminated Wild Turkey from much of its original extensive range, but it is now expanding back into many parts of that original range, helped by modern game management, including restocking programs and careful regulation of hunting.

Northern Bobwhite *Colinus virginianus* 9⁵/₄ in.   **p.168**
Common permanent resident.

The only quail in LBL. The upperparts and upper breast are ruddy brown speckled with gray, black, and white, making the birds difficult to see as they crouch motionless among leaves or grass. The lower breast and belly are buff, scalloped with dark crescents. The sides are coarsely streaked, the tail short and dark. A crest on the top of the head may be laid back, and is then inconspicuous. The bill is short, chicken-like, and black. A broad, blackish stripe passes backward from the base of the bill, beneath the eye, and across the side of the face. The top of the head is brownish-black. Adult males (bird at top in photograph) have a white patch on the upper throat and a white line on the side of the head above the dark facial stripe (in females—bird at bottom in photograph—these areas are buff instead of white). Its loud, clear, whistled, two-note call is of course the basis for its name of bobwhite; when close, a third, faint, introductory note may be heard before the "bob." A single "covey call" note is also given by both sexes. It prefers brushy, open country and avoids dense woodlands. Northern Bobwhite forages and roosts on the ground in small groups called coveys. When roosting, the birds of a covey form a circle with their tails in the center; a ring of droppings then marks the roosting site after they disperse in the morning. They are strong fliers but have little endurance. You may walk nearly upon a covey of several birds, not suspecting their presence until the lot of them explodes like a shell-burst from beneath your feet, leaving you in their wake with your heart in your mouth (I'm still not used to it). The nest is placed on the ground, well-concealed under vegetation.

Virginia Rail *Rallus limicola* 9¹/₄ in.

Rare spring (April to mid-May) and fall (Sept. through Oct.) transient.

Rails are marsh birds with long legs and toes, laterally compressed bodies ("skinny as a rail"), and short tails. Virginia Rail suggests a tiny, long-legged chicken as it slinks among the stems of marsh vegetation, though you can count yourself lucky if you ever actually see one. They are quite secretive and elusive, very reluctant to fly even when pressed, preferring instead to sneak deeper into the concealing vegetation on foot. When they do fly, it seems very labored, and their dangling, long legs make it appear that a landing is imminent—which it usually is (though during migration they move hundreds of miles between their wintering and summering grounds, flying at night). Virginia Rail is rusty brown with dark streaks above; the flanks and undertail coverts are barred black and white. The long, slightly down-curved bill is orange, becoming black toward its tip and along its top. Gray on the side of the face contrasts with a red eye and a short, light stripe in front of the eye. Immatures are similar, but have more black and less rusty below, and darker bills. Rails may vocalize, especially at dawn and dusk, and sometimes at night. Strange squawks, grunts, and squeaks coming from dense, waterside vegetation are likely to be rail sounds. Virginia Rail gives a series of two-syllabled notes, something like "ka-tick, ka-tick, ka-tick," and a laugh-like "wank, wank, wank" (descending in pitch).

Sora *Porzana carolina* 8³/₄ in.

Uncommon spring (late March to late May) and fall (Aug. through Oct.) transient.

About the size of Virginia Rail, but with a much shorter, yellow bill. (See account of Virginia Rail for characteristics of the group.) Adult Soras are mottled brown, black, and white above, with a gray breast and sides of neck and head. The face and throat are black. The lower breast, belly, sides, and flanks are barred with gray, black, and white; undertail coverts are buff. Immatures lack the black on the face and throat, and the gray on breast and sides of neck, being instead buff in those areas. Sora is secretive but not shy, and more likely to forage in the open than other rails, making it easier to see. Like rails generally, Sora can swim, but does so rarely and poorly (the feet are not webbed or lobed). Sora is quicker to flush than other rails, and has the same awkward, gangly appearance in flight when it does. It eats seeds and assorted invertebrates. The common call is a rapid series of "dee" notes, descending in pitch, the whole amounting to a sort of "whinny." It can also whistle—a two-syllabled, ascending "kur-whee."

American Coot *Fulica americana* 15 in.   **p.168**
Permanent resident. Fairly common winter (Sept. through May); rare summer.

This dark bird looks like the offspring of some misbegotten mating between a duck and a chicken, but is actually more closely related to the rails and cranes. An adept swimmer with toes that are large and lobed (rather than webbed as in ducks). The bill is more chickenlike in shape than ducklike, and ashore American Coot walks like a chicken rather than waddles like a duck. Adults (see photograph) are slate gray everywhere except for two white patches beneath the tail, a narrow white stripe on the trailing edge of the wing, and a black head and neck. The bill, which extends up onto the forehead as a sort of shield, is white except for reddish-black spots at the top of the forehead-shield and near the tip of each mandible. The legs and feet are yellowish, the eyes ruby red. Immatures resemble adults but are paler, with grayish bills. American Coot eats many kinds of aquatic plants, algae, small aquatic vertebrates (fish, and amphibian larvae), assorted invertebrates, and sometimes bird eggs. It sometimes dives when feeding. Its calls are many and varied, but a distinctive one is a raucous, deliberate "kuh-kuh-kuh-kuh." Getting airborne requires a long runway of open water along the surface of which they "skitter," foot-splashes in their wake, until they have attained enough air speed to eventually fly.

Black-bellied Plover *Pluvialis squatarola* 12 in.

Extremely rare spring (May), rare fall (late July to mid-Nov.) transient.

Plovers are plump-bodied, thick-necked shorebirds with rather thick bills. Breeding Black-bellied Plover has a black bill, face, throat, breast, belly, legs, and feet. A white forehead is continuous with a white stripe over the eye and down the side of the neck. The undertail coverts are white, and the crown, back, and upper wings are spotted or barred with black and white. The winter plumage is browner above, and lacks the white stripe on head and neck; the underparts are whitish, with faint brown streaking on the breast and sides. The best field mark in winter is the black "wingpit" under each wing, easily seen on the bird in flight as it banks away from you. The wings above are dark, each with a white stripe. The tail is white, finely barred with gray, and the rump is white. The call is a haunting three-syllable whistle, the middle syllable lower pitched. Look for Black-bellied Plover on lake margins, plowed fields, and wet, short grass meadows, where it feeds on a variety of invertebrates. As a typical plover it has the habit, when foraging, of running rapidly for a short distance and then stopping abruptly; it may then probe for food with its bill, or raise its head skyward and take a good look around before repeating the sequence.

Lesser Golden-Plover *Pluvialis dominica* 10^1/$_2$ in.

Rare spring (mid-March to mid-May), extremely rare fall (mid-Aug. to mid-Nov.) transient.

Slightly smaller than Black-bellied Plover, Lesser Golden-Plover is patterned similarly, except as follows: it is much browner above (golden-brown in summer dress), the top of the wing has no white stripe, there is no white rump, the tail above is mostly brown instead of mostly white, and there are no black patches in the "wingpits." It prefers plowed fields and mowed, wet pastures. The call is a two-syllabled, whistled "chew-leak," the second syllable higher. Feeds opportunistically on small invertebrates.

Semipalmated Plover *Charadrius semipalmatus* 7 in.
p.169

Uncommon spring (mid-April through May) and fall (late July to late Oct.) transient.

This small, attractive plover prefers mudflats of lakes and rivers, and flooded, plowed fields (which probably look a lot like mudflats to it). Closely related to Killdeer, it looks like what one might imagine a half-grown Killdeer would. Birds in breeding plumage (see photograph) are un-patterned brown above, with a white stripe on each wing and white lateral borders on the tail. The head is mostly brown, with a white forehead patch, a black face mask, and white on the throat which is continued around the neck as a collar. Below the white throat and collar is a sin-gle black band extending across the upper breast and well onto each side of the neck. The rest of the underparts are pure white. The stubby bill is orange with a black tip, and the legs and feet are orange. Winter birds are similar but have brown on the head, breast, and neck instead of black, a black bill, and dull yellowish legs and feet. The call is an upslurred "chew-eat."

Killdeer *Charadrius vociferus* 10 in. p.169
Permanent resident. Common summer (mid-March to mid-Oct.); fairly common winter.

A robin-sized plover with two black breast bands, seen in LBL, has to be this species. Otherwise it looks much like Semipalmated Plover, but is nearly twice the size, and has an orange rump and base of tail (conspicuous in flight). Killdeer chicks have a single breast band (as in the adult Semipalmated Plover). Killdeer's bill is all black, legs and feet are flesh-colored, and there is a thin, bright red eye-ring. It occurs in open country, often at much greater dis-tances from water than do other shorebirds. May form flocks outside the breeding season, sometimes with other species. Lawns, pastures, and golf courses, as well as mud-flats, sandbars, and lakeshores are all suitable habitats for this species. As the second part of the scientific name sug-gests, Killdeer is indeed vociferous, its loud, piercing "kill-dee, kill-dee, kill-dee," or simply "dee, dee, dee" being among the most familiar bird calls of the region. As nesting sites, Killdeers prefer open expanses of barren ground. Lawns, plowed fields, graveled road shoulders, and parking areas are commonly used, the well-camouflaged eggs being laid in a slight depression ("scrape") in the ground, representing the slightest pretense at nest construction. Injury feigning is a favorite distraction display that the adults of this, and several other birds, use to lure predators away from the nest site. Killdeer may forage, and call, at any time of day or night. Insects are its most important food. Look for the chick and the egg in the photograph.

Greater Yellowlegs *Tringa melanoleuca* 14 in.
Uncommon spring (March through May) and fall (early July to mid-Nov.) transient.

Though Greater Yellowlegs is distinctly larger than Lesser Yellowlegs, the plumage of these two species is nearly identical. When the two are seen together, the size difference is a reliable basis for distinguishing them. But in the case of single birds, or single-species flocks of birds, size is of little use because there is no basis for a comparative assessment of it, and accurate estimates of absolute size are notoriously difficult to make under field conditions. The account of Lesser Yellowlegs gives a basic description of these two species and tips on how to distinguish them (the bill and the voice are the keys). Greater Yellowlegs is less gregarious and a bit more wary of humans than is Lesser, and with its longer legs it can forage in deeper waters. Both yellowleg species sometimes "bob" (tip their heads or tails rapidly up and down) while standing. Feeds on aquatic invertebrates, small fish, tadpoles, and some plant material (berries). Both yellowleg species habitually skim the water's surface for their food, or catch it in the water column, rather than probing the substrate extensively with their bills as many shorebirds do.

Lesser Yellowlegs *Tringa flavipes* 10¹/₂ in.　　p.170
Fairly common spring (March through May) and fall (early June to mid-Nov.) transient.

Lesser Yellowlegs has a body the size of Killdeer's, but has long, bright yellow or yellow-orange legs. Recognizing it as a yellowlegs is easy (Ruff and Upland Sandpiper are the only other long-legged sandpipers with yellow legs that might occur in LBL, but both are extremely rare), but distinguishing it from Greater Yellowlegs is not. Breeding adults of both species are dark brown above, heavily spotted with white. The underparts are white. Head, neck, and breast are finely streaked with gray. In flight, the upper wing surfaces are all dark, the rump is white, and the tail is black-and-white barred. The bill of Lesser Yellowlegs is long (equal to or slightly longer than the head), dark, and straight; in Greater Yellowlegs the bill is similar but even longer (obviously longer than the head), slightly paler on its basal one-third, and typically shows a very slight upward curvature along its entire length (at least along the bottom of the lower mandible). Lesser Yellowlegs has skinnier (i.e., less bulbous) knees than Greater. The call of Lesser Yellowlegs is usually one or two clear, whistled notes: "tew" or "tew, tew"; Greater Yellowlegs' call normally has three or more such notes. Lesser Yellowlegs seems to prefer grassy marshes or ponds to mudflats, though it does occur on mudflats. Diet consists of both aquatic and terrestrial invertebrates, and small fish.

Solitary Sandpiper *Tringa solitaria* 8¹/₂ in.
Fairly common spring (late March to June) and fall (July through Oct.) transient.

The upperparts are dark brown, flecked with small white spots. Underparts are solid white, except for upper breast and neck, which are streaked with gray or brown. The prominent white eye-ring is a good field mark. Both upper and lower wing surfaces are all dark; the distinctive tail is dark down its center, with bold dark-and-white barring on the sides. The bill is straight, fine, and all dark; the legs are greenish. Solitary Sandpiper, true to its name, is usually seen alone, or in very small groups. It is fond of vegetated shorelines along lakes, in marshes, at ponds, or on small streams (even in woodlands). Its darting, swallow-like flight is unlike the stiff-winged flight of Spotted Sandpiper. Solitary Sandpiper has a habit of bobbing its head and tail as it stalks the shallows. The call is a clear, whistled "peet," or "peet-weap," similar to the call of Spotted Sandpiper but higher-pitched.

Spotted Sandpiper *Actitis macularia* 7¹/₂ in.   **p.170**
Summer resident. Fairly common spring (April through
May) and fall (July through Oct.); rare summer.

In breeding plumage (see photograph), this wader is distinctive, both in appearance and behavior. The upperparts
are brown, flecked with black bars and spots. The tail
above is brown toward the center, whitish with dark bars
on the sides. The extended wings show a white stripe
above, and a narrow white line along the trailing edge of
the inner wing. The underparts are white with bold, round,
well-spaced black spots. The brownish head has a dark
eyeline, a broken eye-ring, and a white eyebrow stripe. Bill,
legs, and feet are pinkish or pinkish-orange. Winter birds
are similar but lack the black spots and bars both above
and below, have a less vivid head pattern, a duller bill, and
show a gray patch on the side of the breast, separated by a
short, vertical white bar from the front of the folded wing.
Often seen singly or in very small groups, it is a confirmed
"teeterer." Look for Spotted Sandpiper along almost any
land-water boundary, from lake margins to borders of
small streams and ponds. The "peet-weap" call (second
note often repeated) is similar to the call of Solitary Sandpiper, but lower-pitched. When Spotted Sandpiper flies, its
wing motion is distinctive—rapid, stiff, and mechanical—
the shallow arcs giving the illusion that the bird is flying on
its wing tips.

Ruddy Turnstone *Arenaria interpres* 9 in.
Extremely rare spring (May), rare fall (late July to early
Oct.) transient.

In breeding plumage, this gregarious species is spectacular and distinctive in appearance. Its plumage pattern is
too complex to describe here (see one of the field guides
listed at the end of this book for details), but rufous
above, a white belly, and bold black-and-white patterns on
the head, neck, breast, wings, lower back, rump, and tail
combine to give a harlequin effect, punctuated by a short,
slightly upturned bill and brilliant orange legs and feet.
Winter plumage, the one most likely to be seen in LBL, is
much less striking, being mostly brown above and white
below, with a brown bib that bears a white spot on each

side. Ruddy Turnstone prefers pebbly or gravelly beaches, where it "turns stones" with a quick flick of its bill as it searches for invertebrates hiding beneath. But it will also feed at other types of shorelines, and even in muddy fields. The call is a low, harsh, guttural rattle.

Sanderling *Calidris alba* 7³/₄ in.

Rare fall (mid-July to mid-Oct.) transient. This sandpiper is a confirmed runner along the sandy and gravelly beaches where it forages. Breeding plumage birds (not likely to be seen in LBL) are rusty about the head, neck, and breast, and buff-mottled brown on the back and folded wings. The stout, slightly drooping bill is black at all times, as are the legs and feet. Winter plumage is pale gray above, all white below. The upper wing surface in all plumages has a conspicuous median white stripe on an otherwise dark wing. The tail in flight is dark toward its center, with lighter margins. If you see one Sanderling you are likely to see several, for it is a gregarious species. The call is a sharp "quit."

Semipalmated Sandpiper *Calidris pusilla* 6¹/₄ in.

Fairly common spring (late April through May) and fall (early July through Oct.) transient.

Breeding adults have black or blackish legs, feet, and bill. The bill is straight, no longer than the length of the head, rather stout, and bluntish at its tip (especially in males; female's bill is slightly longer than the male's and shows the faintest droop at its tip). Upperparts are brownish, mottled with buff and black. Underparts are white, the breast and sides finely streaked with brown. Wings above are dark with a narrow, light median stripe. The rump and tail are blackish at their centers and light on their sides. Non-breeding plumage is similar, but grayer above and with reduced streaking on breast and sides. Plumage of Semipalmated Sandpiper is much like that of both Least and Western Sandpipers. Least Sandpiper is slightly smaller, has yellowish or greenish legs and feet, is more definitely streaked on the breast, is browner above, and has a finer, proportionately longer bill. (See account of

Western Sandpiper for tips on how to tell that species from Semipalmated Sandpiper.) Birders use the word "peep" as a collective term for any sparrow-sized sandpiper, and distinguishing among the various species in the field is difficult and sometimes impossible. But it is challenging—some even say fun—and practice at it pays dividends quickly. Mudflats are favorite haunts of this and several other peeps, but it will also work ponds and marshes. Its call is a low, husky "jerk."

Western Sandpiper *Calidris mauri* 6¹/₆ in.
Extremely rare spring (mid-April through May), rare fall (early July through Oct.) transient.

Slightly larger than Semipalmated Sandpiper (see account of that species for a basic description), they look *very* much alike. In adult females at least, the bill of Western Sandpiper is thicker at its base (giving it a more conical, and less tubular, appearance), longer (exceeds head length slightly), and drooped slightly toward its tip. Males may have bills indistinguishable from those of Semipalmated Sandpiper. The call of Western Sandpiper is more like that of Least Sandpiper than of Semipalmated, being a high, rather thin "jeep," or "cheat." It feeds in situations where Semipalmated is likely to occur as well. Beginning birders should not try to identify all the peeps they see to species level. Even expert birders with many years of experience, and under optimum viewing conditions, sometimes must record a small shorebird as simply "peep," or "Western?/Semipalmated?"

Least Sandpiper *Calidris minutilla* 5-3/4 in.　　　p.171
Winter resident. Fairly common spring (April through May) and fall (July through Nov.) transient; rare winter.

Least Sandpiper is indeed the smallest sandpiper of LBL, just by half an inch or so; but half an inch shorter than Semipalmated Sandpiper represents about an eight percent reduction in body length (and an even greater reduction in body mass)—a difference that can generally be discerned when the two species occur together. The plumage of Least Sandpiper is nearly identical to that of Semipalmated and

Western Sandpipers. (See the account of Semipalmated for details, and tips on how to distinguish Least Sandpiper from those species.) Usually seen in groups of several to a few dozen individuals, working the substrate of a wide range of land-water borders, probing excitedly for tiny invertebrates. The call resembles that of Western Sandpiper, a high "creep" or "creet," the vowel often drawn-out.

White-rumped Sandpiper *Calidris fuscicollis* 7³/₄ in.

Rare spring (May to mid-June), extremely rare fall (Aug. through Sept.) transient.

A large peep (peeps being generally the sparrow-sized sandpipers), the white rump, easily seen as the bird flies, makes it relatively easy to identify this species. (Stilt Sandpiper also has a white rump, but is much longer-legged and longer-billed, and has greenish legs.) Otherwise it looks much like Semipalmated Sandpiper (see account of that species for basic description) except it's larger, has longish wings that extend noticeably beyond the tip of the tail when folded, the streaking on its underparts extends well onto the sides (streaks faint in winter plumage), the white rump of course, and, in winter plumage, grayer upperparts. The call of White-rumped Sandpiper is a distinctive, squeaky, high-pitched "tseep," or "jeep." Frequents mudflats, beaches, ponds, and muddy fields, often with other species.

Baird's Sandpiper *Calidris bairdii* 7¹/₄ in.

Extremely rare fall (late July to mid-Oct.) transient.

See the account of Semipalmated Sandpiper for a basic description, which fits Baird's Sandpiper fairly well. Baird's looks much like White-rumped Sandpiper, except that Baird's lacks the all-white rump; is slightly larger; has relatively longer wings (they extend about ¹/₂ inch beyond tip of tail when folded); has a dingier, buffier breast; and, in fall plumage, has a "scalier" appearance above because of buff on the feather edges. The call is a trilled "crreep" or "crrete." The migration route of Baird's Sandpiper is mainly through the Great Plains, so it is an extremely rare bird in the vicinity of LBL.

Pectoral Sandpiper *Calidris melanotos* 8³/₄ in.   **p.171**
Common spring (mid-March through May) and fall (mid-July to early Nov.) transient.

Pectoral Sandpiper is larger and longer-legged than the peeps, and slightly longer-necked. Upperparts are brown, and mottled, streaked, and spotted with black, white, and buff. The belly, flanks, and undertail coverts are white. There is a single, faint stripe on the upper surface of the wing, and a dark, central bar extending from the rump down through the tail; laterally the tail is white at its base and buff toward its tip. The breast is grayish-brown, heavily streaked with dark brown; the streaking stops abruptly at the forebelly, and this sharply demarcated lower breast margin is one of the best field identification marks. The crown often shows some rusty. The legs and feet are yellowish to greenish. The slightly downcurved bill is longer than the head and is lighter in color toward its base than it is near its tip. Pectoral Sandpiper prefers wet, grassy areas to open mud flats. The call is a low-pitched, coarse "cr-rick."

Dunlin *Calidris alpina* 8¹/₂ in.
Rare spring (late April through May), uncommon fall (mid-Aug. to late Nov.) transient.

Dunlin is unmistakable in breeding plumage, with its rufous back and finely streaked underparts with black belly patch. The upper surface of the extended wing is dark, with a median white stripe. The tail above has a dark central bar, white toward the sides at the base, and brown or gray at the outside corners. The bill is black, longer than the head, and droops near its tip. Legs and feet are also black. Winter birds lack the black belly patch and rufous back and are predominantly grayish on the breast and upperparts. Mudflats, sandy beaches, gravelly or rock shores, flooded fields, and grassy pond margins are all used by this species. Its call is a husky, harsh "jeerp," or "greep."

Stilt Sandpiper *Calidris himantopus*

Rare spring (mid-April to late May), uncommon fall (early July through Oct.) transient.

Stilt Sandpiper has long greenish legs and a long, slightly decurved black bill. The breeding adult is dark brown above, mottled with buff. Underparts are light buff with heavy barring. Wings above are dark with only a very faint wing stripe. The rump is white, the tail gray. Stripes on the crown and neck are punctuated by a prominent light eyebrow stripe, bordered above and below by chestnut. Winter birds lack the barring on the underparts, the mottling on the upperparts, and the chestnut on the head. Stilt Sandpiper occurs on muddy lake margins and around ponds and marshes, where it wades in fairly deep water, probing actively and rapidly for crustaceans and other substrate invertebrates. The call is a low, hoarse "wherp."

Buff-breasted Sandpiper *Tryngites subruficollis* 8 in.

Extremely rare fall (early Aug. through Sept.) transient.

Solid-buff face, throat, neck (on front and sides), breast belly, sides, flanks, and undertail coverts contrast with the largely snowy-white underwing surfaces (visible in flight, or as the bird lifts its wings while standing). The upperparts are brown, scalloped with buff or white. Top of head and nape are buff, streaked or speckled with brown, and there is a pale eye-ring. The bill is shorter than the head, blackish (darker toward the tip), and straight. The legs and feet are yellowish. This sandpiper prefers grassy areas when foraging, but may be seen loafing on beaches and gravel bars. Fairly tame, it has an erratic, darting flight when flushed. Its call is a low, rolling trill, followed by a sharp "tik," sometimes repeated.

Short-billed Dowitcher *Limnodromus griseus* 11¼ in.

Rare spring (mid-April to late May), uncommon fall (early July to mid-Oct.) transient.

The two dowitcher species (Long-billed is not described in this book) have very long, stout, straight, blackish bills, and are essentially indistinguishable in the field—especially in the fall—except by voice. Breeding adults of Short-billed Dowitcher are blackish above, mottled with white and buff. The underparts and sides of neck are rufous speckled with black, especially toward the sides. The tail above is black-and-white-barred, fading into a triangular white patch that extends up to mid-back. The wings above are dark with only a faint light stripe on the inner wing. A light eyebrow stripe is bounded above by a dark crown and below by a dark eyeline. Winter birds lack the rufous and are predominantly gray, except for a white belly and undertail coverts. Feeding dowitchers use a rapid, up-and-down, machine-like motion of the head (often with heads underwater) as they probe for food deep into the mud of shallow ponds and marshes. The usual call is a low, two-or-three note whistle: "tew-tew-tew," or "tew-doo."

Common Snipe *Gallinago gallinago* 11 in. p.172
Uncommon winter (Aug. to late May) resident.

Common Snipe likes grassy swales, marshes, and bogs, where it probes in the ground with its very long, straight, dark bill. The upperparts are grayish brown, with four prominent buff-to-white stripes on the back. The head is brown-and-white striped. Brown streaking on the breast changes to barring on the sides, flanks, and undertail coverts; the belly is white. Above, the wings are dark and unstriped, the rump is barred and brownish, and the white-tipped, fan-shaped tail is barred with black and rufous. The rather short legs and feet are grayish-green. A secretive species, Common Snipes tend to be tight sitters, often not flushing when approached until you are nearly upon them; this is especially true where there is much vegetation into which their pattern blends very well. The flight is erratic and zigzag, making them a challenging target for hunters (hence the word "sniper" for one who is a crack shot with a gun). A raspy "zzgape" is commonly uttered as they flush.

American Woodcock *Scolopax minor* 11 in. p.172
Uncommon permanent resident.

A chunky bird with a long, straight bill and short legs. The upperparts are a dead-leaf pattern of brown, gray, black, and white. The top of the head and nape are black, with two prominent, buff crossbars; forehead and face are grayish brown. There is a thin, black eyeline, as well as a black line along the lower margin of the face. Underparts are grayish-buff, cinnamon on the sides and flanks. The tail is very short, with a terminal gray or whitish band. You must get into the field at dawn or dusk in January and February, when this secretive species is making a spectacle of itself by its fascinating courtship rituals, to appreciate the fact that it is not a rare bird (at least at that time of year). The courting male walks about on his "arena" (usually a tiny, open area in brushy, moist situations), giving his nasal "peent" call. After a minute or so of this he takes flight, ascending in a slow, erratic sort of spiral, twittering as he rises. At the flight's zenith, a new group of sounds begins—some vocal, some mechanical (produced by specialized outer primary feathers)—as he plummets erratically toward the ground, slipping and sliding in a zigzag path that carries him back to his arena, where the whole production is begun again. Diet consists largely of earthworms.

Bonaparte's Gull *Larus philadelphia* 13 in.
Uncommon winter (late Sept. to early May) resident.

The smallest gull regularly occurring in LBL. The breeding adult of this beautiful, delicate gull has a black head and bill (a broken, white eye-ring is evident at close range); is all white on its underparts, tail, rump, and back of neck; and has a gray mantle with a conspicuous white, triangular patch toward the tip of each wing on its upper surface. The legs and feet are red. Most birds seen in LBL however are in winter plumage and lack the black head (except for a dark, eye-sized patch over each ear). Bonaparte's Gull does not breed until it is two years old; first year birds have a plumage similar to that of winter adults, but with a black band across the tip of the tail, a dark border on the trailing edge of the wing, a dark bar atop the wing extending diagonally backward from the wrist to the body, and pinkish legs and feet. Gulls seldom dive (terns commonly do), but often swim on the water's surface (terns rarely do).

Ring-billed Gull *Larus delawarensis* 18¹/₂ in.   **p.173**
Fairly common winter (Oct. to early May) resident.

The most common gull of LBL, intermediate in size between the larger Herring Gull and smaller Bonaparte's Gull. Breeding adults (see photograph) have white head, neck, underparts, rump, and tail. The tips of the wings are black, with noticeable white spots; the rest of the mantle is gray. The bill is yellow, with an encircling black ring near its tip. The legs and feet are yellow or greenish-yellow. Winter adults are similar to breeding adults, but have brownish streaks or spots on the head. Ring-billed Gull does not attain full breeding plumage until it is three years old, and immature birds of each age class have a distinctive plumage. (For details on these immature plumages, consult one of the field guides listed at the back of this book.) Ring-billed Gull calls are much like those of Herring Gull, but higher pitched. Gulls are opportunistic feeders and will scavenge extensively when they can. They quickly learn to take advantage of garbage dumps, fish cleaning sites, fish kills, slovenly picnickers and boaters, etc. They may also prey on the eggs and young of other bird species. Aerial kleptoparasitism—the mid-air pirating of food from other species—is sometimes practiced against terns and other gulls. Gulls often loaf in large numbers on favorite bars of islands and headlands.

Herring Gull *Larus argentatus* 24¹/₂ in.
Uncommon winter (Oct. to mid-May) resident.

The largest gull of LBL, this species looks much like Ring-billed Gull (see account of that species for basic description). Breeding Herring Gulls differ from Ring-billed Gulls in being larger, lacking a black ring encircling the bill, and having pinkish or flesh-colored (rather than yellowish) legs and feet. Winter adults have more extensive dusky streaking on the top, sides, and back of the head, back and sides of the neck, and sides of the upper breast than do adult Ring-billed Gulls in winter plumage. Both species commonly occur in the same flock; when they do, the size difference is easily noticed. Herring Gull does not reach full breeding plumage until four years old and, as in Ring-billed and Bonaparte's Gulls, the pre-adult years are each characterized by a distinctive appearance (see one of the field guides listed in the back of this book for details on that complicated subject). A tyrant among gulls, it will eat other birds' eggs and young, or even other adults. It is also an accomplished scavenger and pirate. The call is a loud, strident "kee-ow, kee-ow, kee-ow," or a sort of chuckle, similar to calls of Ring-billed Gull, but lower pitched.

Caspian Tern *Sterna caspia* 21 in.
Uncommon spring (mid-April to late May) and fall (early July to early Oct.) transient.

Caspian Tern is, by far, the largest tern in LBL. Breeding adults are mostly gray above, except for the top half of the head, which is black, and white on the neck. The underparts are white, except for blackish primaries. The large, sharp-pointed bill is coral-red, with some black often visible near its tip; the legs and feet are black. The white tail is notched, but not deeply so. Nonbreeding adults and immatures resemble breeding adults, but have a dusky or streaked (rather than solid black) cap. Terns are marvelous fliers as they cruise or hover over the water, bill pointing downward, watching intently for fish below. When a target is spied, they plunge headfirst after it. It may also pirate fish from other, smaller terns. The voice of Caspian Tern is a harsh, guttural "kraa-ah," or "kraaa."

Common Tern *Sterna hirundo* 14$^{1}/_{2}$ in.
Rare spring (mid-April to mid-May) and fall (mid-July to mid-Oct.) transient.

A graceful, medium-sized tern with a deeply forked tail. Breeding birds are mostly white, with a black cap and nape, a light gray mantle, darkish primaries, red legs and feet, and a red, black-tipped (usually) bill. Immature and non-breeding birds similar, but with the forehead and crown white (nape remains black), the bill, legs and feet dark gray, and with a darkish bar along the upper surface of the wing at its leading edge. It closely resembles Forster's Tern (see account of that species for distinguishing features). Common Tern eats mostly fish, but some invertebrates are taken. Calls include a staccato "kip, kip, kip," and a loud, down-slurred "key-aaarr."

Forster's Tern *Sterna forsteri* 15 in.
Uncommon spring (mid-April to mid-May) and fall (July through Oct.) transient.

Very similar in appearance and behavior to Common Tern (see account of that species for basic description). Breeding birds are best distinguished from Common Tern by primaries that are lighter in color than the rest of the wing (darker in Common Tern), a tail that is gray above except for white borders (tail of Common Tern above is white with dark gray margins), and orange (rather than red) bill, legs, and feet. Winter Forster's Terns have a white forehead and crown and a gray nape (nape is black in winter Common Terns), and lack the dark bar along the leading edge of the top of the wing. The voice is similar to that of Common Tern, but can be distinguished, with experience. Terns can alight on the water and swim, but they are much less likely to do so than are gulls. May scavenge dead fish and capture flying insects, but most of its diet is live fish.

Black Tern *Chlidonias niger* 9¹/₂ in.
Uncommon spring (mid-April through May) and fall (mid-July through Sept.) transient.

A small, dark tern, suggesting a large swallow as it flies low over the water catching insects (its major food) from the air or snatching them from the water's surface. But it will also plunge, tern-like, into the water for small fish— something a swallow would never do. The breeding Black Tern has a black head, neck, breast and belly. The black of the upper neck blends into dark gray on the back, tail, and upper wing surfaces. The undertail coverts are white, and a narrow, white line along the leading edge of the wing may be visible. In winter plumage the underparts are all white (except for a small black patch high on each side of the breast), and the head is whitish on the forehead, gray on top, and has a dark bar on each side through the eye. The tail is slightly notched in all plumages. Immature birds resemble winter adults but are mottled with brown on the wing coverts. Molting birds, changing from winter to breeding plumages, are pied. The call is a shrill "creek," or "geek."

Rock Dove *Columba livia* 12¹/₂ in.
Fairly common permanent resident.

This introduced species, better known to many as the domestic pigeon, is less abundant in LBL now than it was in 1964 when LBL was established. Though it sometimes occurs in remote areas, it seems to prefer human company, and as humans and their structures—in the form of towns, homesteads, and agricultural buildings—disappeared from LBL during its early days, Rock Dove became less common. But it still may be encountered in nearly any open or semiopen area of LBL (though you are most likely to find it near buildings and bridges). There is much variation in plumage color; the most common form is predominantly gray with a white rump and two black bars on the trailing inner wing. The tail is broad and rounded (not pointed, as in Mourning Dove) with a black terminal band. The neck typically has an iridescent green or purple sheen. Grains and other seeds make up most of the diet. The calls are mostly soft, cooing notes. Most nests are found in or on man-made structures such as roofs, ledges, window sills, barn lofts, bridge beams, etc.

Mourning Dove *Zenaida macroura* 12 in.   **p.173**
Common permanent resident.

The only surviving, native dove of LBL (Passenger Pigeon is extinct, and Rock Dove—the domestic pigeon—is not native). A brown or grayish-brown, with a long, pointed tail. The wings and tail are darker than the body, and there are black spots on the inner part of the upper surface of the wings, and a small black spot on each side of the face, behind and beneath the eye. The tips of the tail feathers are white. There is a pink wash on the breast, and a purple iridescence (more prominent in males) on the sides and back of the neck. Immatures are similar, but have spots on the back and breast, and lack the pink and purple on the breast and neck. Found in mature forests, semiopen and brushy areas, grasslands, and agricultural fields. Its diet is almost entirely seeds, and it feeds readily on waste grain left in harvested fields. Not a fastidious homemaker, Mourning Dove builds a skimpy nest well out on a horizontal limb in which it places its two white, unmarked eggs. It may use deserted nests of other species, and occasionally nests on the ground. Very prolific, as many as five broods may be reared in one season (the breeding season is a long one). As in most doves, the hatchlings are fed "crop milk" (secreted by the lining of a portion of the esophagus) for the first few days of their lives. The call is a beautiful, mournful "who-woo, who, who who" the second syllable—the "woo"—higher pitched. In spite of substantial hunting pressure from humans, Mourning Dove is doing quite well, even expanding its range in recent decades.

Black-billed Cuckoo *Coccyzus erythropthalmus* 12 in. Rare spring (late April through May), extremely rare fall (early Sept. to mid-Oct.) transient.

A long-tailed, long-billed bird, brown above and white below. Looks much like Yellow-billed Cuckoo, but has a black (instead of yellow) lower mandible, an orange-red eye-ring (you must be close to see it), narrow white bars across the undersurface of the tail, and lacks conspicuous rufous in the primary feathers. Immatures similar, but have a yellowish eye-ring, are slightly buff underneath—especially on the throat and undertail coverts—and have less-prominent white bars on the underside of the tail. Cuckoos eat a variety of plant and animal fare (including lizards, salamanders, frogs, various berries and fruits, snails, and bird's eggs), but they specialize on fuzzy caterpillars—especially tent caterpillars. The call of Black-billed Cuckoo is a soft, monotone "coo-coo-coo, coo-coo-coo, coo-coo-coo" (sometimes in groups of four instead of three); the grouping of the notes into threes or fours is fairly distinctive from the call of Yellow-billed Cuckoo.

Yellow-billed Cuckoo *Coccyzus americanus* 12 in. **p.174**
Common summer (mid-April through Oct.) resident.
Woodlands and thickets are the preferred habitat of this

species, the common cuckoo of LBL during the summer months. In appearance it looks much like Black-billed Cuckoo but differs in having a yellow lower mandible, no orange-red eye-ring, six large white spots (instead of narrow white bars) on the underside of the tail, and conspicuous rufous patches in the primaries (easily seen when the bird flies). The distinctive call is a long series of "cuc" notes, the notes initially short and very close together, but becoming slower and more widely spaced as the song progresses: "cu-cu-cu-cu-cu-cu-ca-ca-ca-ca-ca-cow-cow-cow-cowlp-cowlp-cowlp." Loves fuzzy caterpillars, and trees infested with tent caterpillars are favorite feeding spots. A shy bird, it is usually noticed as it flies low across the road or from thicket to thicket, its rufous wing patches flashing. Seems to sing more readily on cloudy days, which accounts for its local common name of "rain crow."

Eastern Screech-Owl *Otus asio* 8¹/₂ in.   **p.174**
Uncommon permanent resident.

This small, "eared" owl comes in two color phases—red and gray (see photograph). In LBL, the red (or rufous) phase is much more common than the gray, but the ratio of the two phases varies geographically. The color of the bird is determined genetically, and is not related to either the age or the sex of the individual. In both color phases the background color is speckled, streaked, and spotted with black and white. The feather tufts, or "ears," are set well apart, and may be erected or laid flat against the head. The eyes are yellow, and the facial disc is rimmed in black. An opportunistic carnivore, Eastern Screech-Owl will eat insects, small birds and mammals, frogs, lizards, snakes, fish, and crayfish, depending on what is most available and catchable. Like owls generally, bones, feathers, hair, and invertebrate exoskeletons are not digested but are instead regurgitated in well-formed pellets which accumulate beneath favorite roosts. Nests are usually in cavities of tree limbs, but nest boxes are sometimes used. The daylight hours are typically passed in tree cavities, but dense, concealing vegetation near a tree trunk will also serve. The call is a rapid, tremulous whinny, first rising, then falling in pitch; it also produces a monotone trill. Prefers semiopen habitat.

70

Great Horned Owl *Bubo virginianus* 22 in.   **p.175**

Uncommon permanent resident.

A large, gray-brown owl with yellow eyes, black bill, and prominent, widely spaced ear tufts, seen in LBL, is sure to be this species. The gray-brown of the back is mottled. From the front, a white throat patch is visible. The tawny-brown facial discs are bordered by black "parentheses." As in all "eared" owls, the feather tufts atop the head may be inconspicuous when laid back, as they are likely to be in flight. Immatures similar to adults, but with smaller ear tufts and redder plumage. Females are distinctly larger than males as adults (a characteristic of many raptors). Great Horned Owl is one of the earliest nesters in LBL, often beginning its nesting activities in mid-winter. Incubation begins with the laying of the first egg, so hatching is staggered over several days; a nest therefore typically contains owlets of distinctly different sizes, and in times of food scarcity the older, larger nestlings are at a distinct advantage. Great Horned Owl usually nests in old hawk (occasionally squirrel) nests, and may use the same nest for several years. A fierce predator, it specializes on rabbits and rodents, but also takes snakes (including venomous ones), birds (including other owls), insects, fish, and even house cats. The call is a soft, low "who, who, who-who-who, whooo, whooo," the middle notes typically run together. Occurs in a wide variety of wooded habitats, including urban areas.

Barred Owl *Strix varia* 21 in.   **p.175**

Fairly common permanent resident.

Slightly smaller than Great Horned Owl, Barred Owl is predominantly grayish-brown, with white bars over the back and the upper surfaces of wings and tail. The underparts are basically buff, with brown barring on the breast contrasting sharply with brown streaking on the belly. Barred Owl lacks ear tufts, has a yellowish bill, and soft brown eyes. A woodland owl, it prefers river bottoms, ravines, and moist lower slopes. It sometimes hunts during mid-day, especially in overcast weather conditions. Feeds largely on mice and other small mammals, but will also take reptiles, amphibians, insects, and birds. Commonly nests in abandoned hawk nests. Owls have excellent night vision, and their large eyes are immovably fixed in their sockets, making it necessary for the bird to continuously turn its head in order to keep its gaze fixed on a moving object; the head can be rotated on the flexible neck through about three-quarters of a full circle. Owls also tend to have keen hearing, and a silent, moth-like flight (the outer edges of the outermost primary feathers are fringed, which helps to muffle the sound of the beating wings). Barred Owl is quite vocal, and when a family group just off the nest starts wailing, hooting, and growling it sounds like a real cat fight. The usual call is a loud, low "who, who, who-whoo, who who, who-whoo-aaaw," the "aaaw" lower pitched; sometimes only part of the full call is given, but the "aaaw" note is almost always included and is quite diagnostic.

Common Nighthawk *Chordeiles minor* 9$\frac{1}{2}$ in. **p.176**
Fairly common spring (mid-April to late May) and fall (late Aug. to early Oct.) transient; rare summer resident.

The "bullbat" to local residents, Common Nighthawk is the most aerial of the three goatsuckers of LBL. (The name "goatsucker" comes from an ancient legend, going back at least to the time of Aristotle, which holds that these birds feed by sucking milk from goats' udders. Bullbat doo-doo, dear reader! The human imagination is indeed fertile.) As is typical of goatsuckers (Whip-poor-will and Chuck-will's-widow are the other members of this group found in LBL), it is well camouflaged for its habit of roosting lengthwise on horizontal tree limbs and nesting on the ground. Common Nighthawk is a mottled grayish-brown above. The very long wings reach the tip of the tail when folded, are mostly black from the wrist out, and each bears a conspicuous white bar halfway between the wrist and the primary tips, running from the leading to the trailing edge of the wing. Adult males (see photograph) have a white upper throat, and a white band across the tail just before the tip. Females and immatures resemble adult males, but lack the white tail band, and have buff-colored (in immatures, sometimes mottled) throats. An accomplished flier, Common Nighthawk is usually detected overhead, at any hour of the day or night, as it winds along on easy wingbeats, catching insects. During fall migration, large flocks assemble and wheel through the air in lazy circles, feeding on insects as they drift southward. A favored nesting site is atop flat-roofed buildings. The call is a nasal "peent," uttered repeatedly in flight.

Chuck-will's-widow *Caprimulgus carolinensis* 12 in.
Uncommon summer (mid-April through Aug.) resident.

This large goatsucker (the group is also known as "nightjars") looks much like Whip-poor-will, but has more reddish brown above, a buffier head, and a brown (rather than black) throat above the white collar (collar is buff in females). Though the adult male shows white in his spread tail, there is less of it than in Whip-poor-will's tail, and it is restricted to the inner half of each of the three outer tail feathers; the effect is one of a brown-and-white-striped outer portion of the tail, rather than white corner patches as in the tail of Whip-poor-will. The songs of the two species are similar, but not confusingly so. There are more syllables (usually four, but five when the first is given twice), in Chuck-will's-widow's song. My grandfather, who lived in the Missouri Ozarks, knew these two species as "whip-poor-will" and "chip-off-a-white-oak," based on differences in their songs. The habits and habitats of the two species are similar, but Chuck-will's-widow tends to feed on larger insects, including the large nocturnal moths of the area, and even, occasionally, small songbirds such as warblers.

Whip-poor-will *Caprimulgus vociferus* 9¹/₂ in.   p.176
Common summer (April through Sept.) resident.

The wings of this woodland goatsucker are shorter (when folded they stop well short of the tail tip) and more rounded than those of Common Nighthawk, and it lacks white wing patches. The upperparts are a mottled mixture of brown, gray, and black, making Whip-poor-will nearly invisible when roosting or incubating eggs on the leaf-littered forest floor. The adult male has a blackish throat above a white collar, and the terminal halves of the outer three tail feathers on each side are white (collar and tail patches are buff in the female). (See account of Chuck-will's-widow for tips on distinguishing that species from Whip-poor-will.) Whip-poor-will feeds by catching insects on the wing, but stays much nearer the ground when doing so than does Common Nighthawk, and it does not feed in daylight. The camouflaged eggs are laid on the open forest floor atop fallen leaves. The song is so well-known, and adequately rendered by the bird's common name, that it needs little description. At close range a soft, muffled note may be heard preceding the "whip" of the regular three-syllabled song. The song may be given in rapid succession dozens, or even hundreds, of times without pause during the height of the breeding season.

Chimney Swift *Chaetura pelagica* 5¹/₄ in.   **p.177**
Common summer (early April to early Oct.) resident.

Chimney Swift, which suggests a swallow but is actually more closely related to hummingbirds, is a dark, sooty gray everywhere (lighter on the throat and upper breast). The wings are built for speed—long, narrow, swept back, and pointed—and extend way beyond the tip of the short, spiny tail when folded (see photograph; when the bird is perched, the tail is used as a prop, woodpecker-fashion, to support its weight). This most aerial of all LBL's birds does almost everything on the wing. It feeds on flying insects, collects twigs for nest building by flying low over the ground and snatching them with its beak, drinks by skimming over the water's surface as it dips its lower bill into the water, courts and mates in mid-air, and probably even takes short naps aloft (based on the reports of some glider pilots). The feet are tiny, and useless for any purpose other than clinging to the wall of some vertical surface, such as the inside of a chimney, hollow tree trunk, silo, cistern, etc., where the birds roost at night and when they build their nests. The nest is made of twigs, glued together and stuck to the sides of their nesting retreats by a sticky salivary secretion. (The flavor of bird's nest soup, a delicacy in parts of the Orient, comes from the nests of the Edible Swiftlets of Borneo and Indonesia. Those nests are made almost entirely of dried saliva. I have not tried Chimney

Swift's-nest soup.) Nesting often occurs in small colonies in preferred sites. The call is a series of rapid, chattering notes, uttered frequently in flight. They will feed wherever there are flying insects.

Ruby-throated Hummingbird *Archilochus colubris*
3¹/₂ in.   p.177
Common summer (mid-April to early Oct.) resident.

This tiniest of all birds in LBL is, surprisingly, a fairly close relative of Chimney Swift (though in different families, they are members of the same order—sort of "cousins," you might say). The adult male (see photograph) is iridescent emerald green above, with a blackish tail and a long, needle-like black bill. The ruby-red throat patch may appear black under certain lighting conditions. The rest of the underparts are whitish, except for some gray or greenish-gray on the sides. Females and immatures resemble adult males, but have white throats and white tips on their outer tail feathers. Their ability to fly in any direction (forward, backward, up, down, or sideways), and to hover motionless before a flower for seconds on end as they probe the nectaries with their long bills and even longer tongues, has earned hummingbirds the nickname "helicopters of the bird world." Besides flower nectar, they eat small insects and spiders, and occasionally tree sap from woodpecker holes. The beautiful, lichen-bedecked, down-lined, golfball-sized nest is held together with spider's silk; it looks like a miniature version of Blue-gray Gnatcatcher's nest, and may be used for more than one year. Besides the high, squeaky, chattering sounds that are often given in flight, the wings, beating at about 50 beats per second, produce a distinctive humming or whirring sound. When my children were in elementary school in Stewart County, Tennessee in the mid-1960s, they were assured by their principal that hummingbirds assaulted soaring vultures, diving at the huge birds from above, impaling them with their long bills, thus killing them. I don't know how widespread this legend is.

Belted Kingfisher *Ceryle alcyon* 13 in.   **p.178**
Fairly common permanent resident.

Belted Kingfisher is blue-gray above and on the head with a white spot before each eye; the white throat extends well up onto the sides of the neck, producing a "collared" look. The blue-gray of the back extends as a broad band across the breast. In males the belly is all white, but in females a rusty band crosses the belly and extends down the sides, separated from the breast band by a white strip; Belted Kingfisher is thus one of those rare bird species in which the female is more colorful than the male. This big-headed bird with its frowsy crest is typically found near water, but it's not very particular about the size of the body of water— anything from Kentucky Lake to a small, isolated pond not 30 feet across will do—as long as there are fish in it. It captures fish by plunging from above, either from a perch or from a hovering position, usually completely disappearing underwater, only to emerge a few seconds later with a fish in its bill (it does not impale the fish, though its sharply pointed bill would seem suited to that task). The call is a loud, staccato rattle. The nest is at the rear of a long (two to four foot) burrow that is excavated in the face of a vertical mud or gravel bank.

Red-headed Woodpecker *Melanerpes erythrocephalus*
8³/₄ in.   **p.178**
Uncommon permanent resident.

This red, white, and blue (actually, blue-black) bird has been called the "All-American Woodpecker." The head, neck, and throat of adults (see photograph) are all red. Underparts and rump are snowy white, and there is a large white patch on the inner, trailing edge of each wing. The rest of the wings, the back, and the tail are blue-black. Immatures have brown, finely streaked heads, and are brown (variously streaked and barred) in those places where the adults are blue-black. The underparts of immatures are a dingy white, faintly streaked with brown. Red-headed Woodpecker prefers semiopen areas rather than dense forests. It is a conspicuous species, often perching on exposed dead snags, and frequently giving its loud, high-pitched "queer" call. Besides insects and spiders, it feeds on various nuts and berries, which it may cache in natural cavities for later consumption. Though often found near stream margins and beaver ponds, it is not restricted to such places. It is loosely colonial, and where one is found others are likely to be also; yet, between the colonies, there may be extensive areas of apparently suitable habitat with no Red-headed Woodpeckers. In recent decades Red-headed Woodpecker has suffered a population decline in many parts of its range. The reasons for this decline are unclear, but competition with the wide-ranging and aggressive European Starling for nest cavities is one possibility.

Red-bellied Woodpecker *Melanerpes carolinus* 9¹/₄ in.

p.179

Common permanent resident.

Any woodpecker seen in LBL that has a black-and-white-barred back, and red on the back of the head and neck is this species (though immatures lack the red). In adult males, red also covers the crown, extending forward to the base of the bill; in adult females (see photograph) the crown is gray, and there is just a touch of orange on the front of the head, above the bill base. The black-and-white barring of the back extends onto the inner half of the wings; the outer half of each wing is black with a white "window" toward the front. Underparts and sides of the head and neck are light gray, and there is a reddish wash on the belly (seldom visible in the field, but conspicuous on birds lying belly-up in a museum tray). Juveniles have streaked breasts. Wherever there are trees in LBL Red-bellied Woodpecker is likely to be also, from lakeside to ridgetop, in both mature woodlands and semiopen, park-like areas. A common call note is similar to that of Red-headed Woodpecker, but is lower-pitched and softer; a rattle-like call is also given.

Yellow-bellied Sapsucker *Sphyrapicus varius* 8¹/₄ n.

Uncommon winter (late Sept. to mid-May) resident.

The only woodpecker in LBL not present year-round. Adult male has a bold pattern of black and white stripes on the head and neck, with a red forehead patch and red throat. The breast sports a black bib, but is otherwise a pale sulphur yellow. Dark spots and bars adorn the sides and flanks. A broad white stripe on the inner wing, visible as a "shoulder patch" when the wings are folded, is a good field mark in all plumages. The back is black-and-light barred, the rump white. Females have a white (instead of red) throat patch, and immatures lack red on the head, and have a brownish back. Yellow-bellied Sapsucker occurs in a variety of forested habitats, where it betrays its presence by drilling regular patterns of shallow holes in a wide variety of native tree species (well over 200 species of woody plants have been reported as having been "tapped"). These holes, made into the cambium layer of living wood, then ooze sap which is consumed by Yellow-bellied Sapsucker on a return visit. Often the holes are arranged as horizontal rows around the trunk, but other patterns—including rectangular grids—may be seen. Besides sap, insects—including some attracted to or trapped by the oozing sap—are eaten, as well as berries and nuts. The holes may serve as routes of fungal infection on the tree, though most trees seem little affected. Rather quiet for a woodpecker, at least during its stay in LBL, it does have a down-slurred, mewing note, rather soft, and with a nasal quality.

Downy Woodpecker *Picoides pubescens* 6¹/₂ in. **p.179**
Common permanent resident.

The smallest woodpecker of LBL, Downy Woodpecker has solid white underparts, and is black and white above. The head has a black crown, forehead, cheek patch, and mustache line. The back of the neck is black, and the back has a large white center bordered with black. The wings are black with rows of white spots, and the rump is black. White outer feathers on an otherwise black tail are studded with black dots (these dots are absent in the similar Hairy Woodpecker). The adult male (see photograph) has a red nape patch. Best distinguished from Hairy Woodpecker by smaller size (Hairy Woodpecker is the size of Red-bellied Woodpecker), and proportionately smaller bill (Downy Woodpecker's bill looks puny even for a puny woodpecker). With experience, the two species may be easily distinguished by their call notes: a soft "pick" in the case of Downy Woodpecker, compared to the sharper, louder "peak" in the case of Hairy Woodpecker. Both species give a Kingfisher-like rattle call as well, but Downy Woodpecker's is higher pitched. Feeds mostly on insects, but also eats various fruits, berries, seeds, and nuts. Sometimes seen clinging, chickadee-style, upside-down at the tip of a small branch as it works to extract seeds.

Hairy Woodpecker *Picoides villosus* 9 in.   **p.180**
Fairly common permanent resident.

A larger version of Downy Woodpecker. (See account of that species for description, and information on how to distinguish between the two.) Though probably never as abundant as Downy Woodpecker, Hairy Woodpecker populations seem to be declining over much of this species' range. No one knows why. Hairy Woodpecker is more restricted to forests than is Downy Woodpecker, or at least to larger trees. Larvae of wood boring beetles are its most important dietary item. It will also (and this is true of several other species as well) feed on the sap, and insects attracted to the sap, of Yellow-bellied Sapsucker holes. The eggs are unblemished white, as the eggs of hole-nesting species typically are; there is no selective advantage in camouflaging eggs only to place them in dark, secluded places, hidden from visually oriented predators. The tongue, as in most woodpeckers, is long, barbed, sticky, and quite protrusible—near-perfect for extracting reluctant insects from deep recesses.

Northern Flicker *Colaptes auratus* 12¼ in.   **p.180**
Fairly common permanent resident.

A large woodpecker, the back and wings are brown above, prominently barred with black. The top of the head and back of the neck are all gray, but for a red crescent on the nape. Throat, upper breast, and sides of neck are brown, except for a prominent black mustache mark in the adult male (see female in photograph). A black patch crosses the upper breast; the rest of the breast, and the sides, flanks, belly, and undertail coverts are light tan to buff, with numerous scattered black spots. Undersurfaces of the wings and tail are yellow. A conspicuous white rump patch is a good field mark as the bird flies away from you. Though it spends much of its time in trees, Northern Flicker may also be seen on the ground—even in open grassy areas—probing for ants, which it seems to find particularly delectable. Flocks of several, or a few dozen, birds may be seen during the nonbreeding season. The call is a loud, rapid "lik, lik, lik, lik, lik, lik, lik," similar to the call of Pileated Woodpecker, but faster, longer, slightly higher-pitched, and not as loud (but still pretty loud). Another call is a distinctive "klee-ear," the second note lower-pitched.

Pileated Woodpecker *Dryocopus pileatus* 17¹/₂ in. **p.181**
Fairly common permanent resident.

The giant among LBL woodpeckers, Pileated Woodpecker is not likely to be confused with any other local species. Log god and hen-of-the-woods are among the more colorful colloquial names for this species. The larger Ivory-billed Woodpecker, which may have occurred in primeval riverbottom forests along the Tennessee and Cumberland rivers in what is today LBL, is almost certainly extirpated in the U.S. (a few individuals still exist in Cuba). The back, wings, tail, and rump are solid black above, except for some white at the base of the flight feathers (noticeable only when the bird's wings are extended). The underparts are also black. Extensive white wing linings underneath are continuous with a white stripe extending up each side of the neck to join with a white facial stripe. The lower throat is black, the upper throat white. Adult males (see photograph) have a prominent, flaming red crest, the red continuing over the crown to the base of the upper bill; there is also a red patch on each side of the face behind the base of the lower bill. Females have red only on the crest and back of the crown. Though most common in woodlands, Pileated Woodpecker also frequents fairly open situations, so long as there are some large trees or tree stumps available and a substantial woodland nearby. The entrance to the nest cavity is larger and more oval than those of other LBL woodpeckers. Its call is similar to that of Northern Flicker, but louder, slower, shorter, and lower-pitched. Carpenter ants are a favorite food, and the birds will excavate large holes, up to eight inches deep, to get at the ant colonies. They also take wood boring beetles, both larvae and adults.

Olive-sided Flycatcher *Contopus borealis* 7^1/$_2$ in.
Rare spring (May) and fall (mid-Aug. through Sept.) transient.

A big, large-headed, heavy-billed, rather short-tailed flycatcher, Olive-sided Flycatcher is usually seen perched high in a dead snag near an opening in the woods or beside a beaver pond, singing its distinctive "quick, three beers" (second note highest) song. Adult birds are brownish-olive above and on the sides of the breast. The white throat continues as a white streak down the center of the breast to the white belly. There are no wing bars, but two tufts of white feathers from the lower back may protrude from behind the wings. Though often hidden by the folded wings, these white tufts are unique among LBL flycatchers. The bill is black, except for some yellow toward the base of the lower mandible. Immatures look like adults, but are darker. Feeds on flying insects, especially bees and wasps.

Eastern Wood-Pewee *Contopus virens* 6 in. p.181
Common summer (mid-April to mid-Oct.) resident.

Eastern Wood-Pewee is best distinguished from the slightly larger Eastern Phoebe by its light lower mandible (at least in adults) and two narrow, white wing bars. From the smaller "empids" (flycatchers of the genus *Empidonax*), it may be distinguished by its lack of an eye-ring, and larger size. The songs of Eastern Wood-Pewee and Eastern Phoebe are easily distinguishable; the former's song is a clear (not raspy, as in Eastern Phoebe), whistled, "pee-a-wee" (second note lowest, last note drawn out and slurred upward), or "pee-wee" (second note lower), or an upslurred "pweeee." Though both species occur in forested or brushy places, Eastern Wood-Pewee is less restricted to the vicinity of water or moist conditions. The well-camouflaged nest is typically placed at middle levels of the forest, on a horizontal limb, well away from the trunk. Like many flycatchers, it is a perch-and-sally feeder: it perches on a limb with a commanding view of the surrounding air space, sallies after passing insects, and usually returns to its perch to eat them.

Acadian Flycatcher *Empidonax virescens* 5³/₄ in. **p.182**
Common summer (mid-April to early Oct.) resident.

Four species of flycatchers found in LBL are members of the genus *Empidonax* (commonly called "empids" by birders). All are small, have two whitish wing bars, a light eyering, and are notoriously difficult to distinguish visually (though their voices and habitat preferences are fairly distinctive). For details on the finer points of identifying these flycatchers visually—sometimes a daunting task even for experienced birders—consult one of the field guides listed at the back of this book. Acadian Flycatcher is by far the most common empid in LBL, and the only one likely to be encountered there in June and July (but see Willow Flycatcher). Acadian Flycatcher prefers deciduous woodlands, especially ravines and moist, lower slopes. The song is an explosive, loud, two-syllabled "pete-zeek," the second syllable longer, burry, and rising in pitch. The shallow nest is coarsely constructed of bark, weeds, twigs, etc., suspended between two twigs well out on a horizontal limb, typically 5 to 20 feet above the ground.

Alder Flycatcher *Empidonax alnorum* 6 in.
Rare spring (May) transient.

An "empid," Alder Flycatcher is virtually identical to Willow Flycatcher in appearance (the two used to be considered a single species; see account of Acadian Flycatcher for general remarks on distinguishing between different empid species). Both have only faint eye-rings. Alder Flycatcher prefers wetter, less open habitats than does Willow Flycatcher, though during migration differences in habitat preference are weaker than on the breeding grounds. But their typical songs are different—Alder Flycatcher's song is a burry, three-syllabled, "vee be-oh," the second syllable accented, and the transition from the second to the third syllable indistinct or slurred.

Willow Flycatcher *Empidonax traillii* 5³/₄ in.

Rare summer (early May through Aug.) resident.

Though this species has not yet been documented as a breeding bird of LBL, it may soon be, based on what is known of its activities in Kentucky and Tennessee. Nests have recently been reported from southern Stewart and Henry counties in Tennessee, and the past few decades have seen a rather steady growth in the known breeding range of the species. It looks just like Alder Flycatcher (and pretty much like all the other empids of LBL—see account of Acadian Flycatcher), but has a distinctive song: a sneezy "fits-bew," the accent on the first syllable, the second syllable down-slurred. It prefers thickets, especially near water. Look for it in dense willow stands, river bottom marshes, and around beaver ponds. The eye-ring, characteristic of empids generally, is faint in this species (as in Alder Flycatcher).

Least Flycatcher *Empidonax minimus* 5¹/₄ in.   **p.182**
Fairly common spring (late April to late May), uncommon fall (late Aug. to early Oct.) transient.

The smallest flycatcher in LBL, Least Flycatcher is a typical "empid" (it has a conspicuous eye-ring and two white wing bars —see account of Acadian Flycatcher). The song is vigorous and distinctive: a crisp, two syllabled "she-beck," with the second syllable accented and usually higher-pitched. Occurs in semiopen areas, along woodland edges, and in park-like habitats. Not as given to choosing conspicuous calling perches as are many other flycatchers, its presence is usually noted by its charactcristic call coming from the middle to upper branches of the trees in which it forages for insects.

Eastern Phoebe *Sayornis phoebe* 6³/₄ in.   **p.183**
Permanent resident. Common summer (March through Oct.), uncommon winter (Nov. through Feb).

The adult is dark gray-brown above, lacking wing bars and eye-ring. The underparts are3 pale gray, slightly darker on the breast. The entire bill is black. Immature birds are similar to adults, but have faint, buff wing bars and a yellowish wash on underparts. It has the habit of bobbing its tail when perched. Prefers forested areas, near water. The nest contains much mud, and is typically festooned with bits of moss and lichen on its exterior; it is constructed on a ledge, or plastered to a vertical surface beneath rock overhangs, bridges, culverts, porches, etc. Most bridges and culverts in LBL have an Eastern Phoebe nest under or in them each summer, sometimes in close proximity to Barn Swallow nests. The bird hawks insects in the middle layers of the vegetation near its nest. Its namesake song is a raspy, "fee-bee," or "fee-bree," repeated often, with the second syllable alternately higher and then lower-pitched than the first.

Great Crested Flycatcher *Myiarchus crinitus* 8 in. **p.183**
Common summer (mid-April to mid-Sept.) resident.

The largest flycatcher found regularly in LBL (there is one record of the larger Scissor-tailed Flycatcher from LBL), this species prefers the canopy of forests. Its back, top of head, and back of neck are olive brown. The tail is russet, and the wings, especially in flight, also show much russet. There are two light-colored, indistinct wing bars on each wing. The bright yellow belly contrasts with a gray breast and throat. Great Crested Flycatcher nests in natural cavities, woodpecker holes, and birdhouses (including martin houses). The bulky nest contains leaves, feathers, discarded bits of paper, snakeskins, etc. A noisy bird, it is easily heard but difficult to see. The common call is a loud, breezy, "wheerp," or "purr-eet." It feeds on insects that it seeks in the forest canopy or gleans from bark; it will also take an occasional small lizard, and eats some berries.

Eastern Kingbird *Tyrannus tyrannus* 8¹/₂ in.   **p.184**
Common summer (early April to mid-Sept.) resident.

In semiopen country, along woodland edges, and in overgrown fields, look for Eastern Kingbird near the top of some convenient perch. It is dark gray above, except for a white band across the tip of its black tail and an orange or red crown patch (usually concealed except when the bird is excited). The underparts are white, with a light gray or dusky breast sometimes evident. The two light wing bars are not conspicuous. As in many flycatchers, the top of the head in profile may have a rough, angular appearance, suggestive of a slight crest. The nest is typically placed high in an isolated tree. Eastern Kingbird is fearless and aggressive and will attack large raptors in flight. I once saw one land on the back of a flying Red-tailed Hawk and proceed to peck vigorously at the hawk's feathers. They will defend their nests aggressively against intruders, even humans. Eastern Kingbird eats flying insects primarily, but also some berries. The call is loud, high-pitched, and harsh, either a single note or a rapid series of notes run together as a sort of chatter. Also a raspy "tzeeb."

Horned Lark *Eremophila alpestris* 7¹/₂ in.   p.184

Permanent resident. Uncommon winter (Oct. through May), extremely rare summer.

An open country species, look for Horned Lark on barren ground, stubble fields, and large, closely mowed grasslands. In such places it walks hurriedly over the ground in search of invertebrates and seeds. Where you see one Horned Lark you are likely to see several or many—even hundreds. The bird is brown above, faintly streaked on the back. The tail is black, except for white outer feathers which show best in flight. Underparts are pale buff to whitish, faintly streaked towards the sides and upper breast. The striking pattern of the head and neck is diagnostic. A yellow throat is bordered below by a black bib on the upper breast, and on the sides by a broad, black mustache. A white forehead patch extends back over the eyes as an eyebrow stripe. Above the eyebrow stripe is a black line that continues across the face and terminates posteriorly in the "horns" (the black "horns" are, of course, feather tufts, and are often difficult to see). The top of the crown is brown. Females and immatures resemble males, but are less vivid. A true lark, Horned Lark sings a song worthy of its family's tradition: a jumbled series of high-pitched, tinkling notes. During courtship, the male sings aloft, circling and rising hundreds of feet as he repeatedly sings his merry song; at the zenith of his flight he hovers, sometimes for several minutes, before folding his wings and plummeting, stonelike, toward the earth, braking his freefall just before impact.

Purple Martin *Progne subis* 7³/₄ in. **p.185**
Common summer (mid-March through Aug.) resident.
The largest of the six species of swallows of LBL. The adult male is a deep purple all over, except for nearly black wings and tail. The tail is notched, but not deeply forked. A short, broad bill, typical of swallows, is adapted to foraging on flying insects. Females (see photograph) and immatures have grayish underparts and are dull purple above. Highly aerial, Purple Martin is a colonial cavity nester. Originally a tree cavity nester, today almost all Purple Martins (in the East, at least) use man-made houses of several to many compartments. Gourds, of the appropriate size and with a hole provided, may also be hung from tiered poles or wires to attract a colony of Purple Martins. Once a colony has become established, it tends to persist year after year, as long as the houses remain usable. The song becomes a pleasantly familiar sound of summer to anyone spending much time in the vicinity of a Purple Martin colony. It is a melodic, liquid gurgle, with a few twitters often thrown in toward the end. Though it may feed over woodlands, water, grasslands, or brushy areas, it seems to prefer nesting houses located in semiopen or open areas which provide unobstructed flight space nearby.

Tree Swallow *Tachycineta bicolor* 5¹/₂ in. **p.185**
Summer resident. Common spring (late March to early May) and fall (late Aug. to mid-Oct.), rare summer.
A distinctly two-toned (as *bicolor* suggests) swallow. Adult male (see photograph) is glossy greenish- to bluish-black above, including wings and tail, but usually just looks black at a distance or in any light except full sunlight. Underparts are pure white; the tail is notched. Adult female is similar, but duller. Immatures are dark grayish-brown above. Tree Swallow is usually seen in LBL during its migration, flying in circles over water or wet meadows, feeding on aerial insects. An early spring migrant, it may feed on berries if cold spells keep insects grounded.

86

Nests—sometimes in loose colonies—in cavities of dead trees and snags, near or over water (will also use bird boxes). After the breeding season, large flocks of this and certain other swallow species may assemble on utility lines and fences. Gregarious birds, they tend to migrate in loose flocks (during the day, as do all our swallows). A distinctive high-pitched "kleet" or "klweet" is frequently uttered during flight.

Northern Rough-winged Swallow *Stelgidopteryx serripennis* 5¹/₂ in.

Fairly common summer (late March through Sept.) resident.

A brown-backed swallow, with dingy throat and upper breast, a notched tail, and lacking a distinct breast band. Less gregarious than our other swallows, both during migration and as a nester. Nests in burrows in banks, or crevices in road cuts and beneath bridges and culverts, sometimes far from the nearest water. It feeds largely on flying insects, but will occasionally take them from the ground. The call note is a harsh, grating "brrit."

Bank Swallow *Riparia riparia* 5 in.

Summer resident. Uncommon spring (early April to mid-May) and fall (Aug. through Sept.), rare summer.

Our smallest swallow. Brown above, white body beneath, with a distinct brown band across the upper breast contrasting with the white throat (Rough-winged Swallow has a dusky throat). The tail is notched. A colony nester in burrows of vertical or near-vertical dirt or gravel banks, along or near water. Compared to other swallows, its flight is swift and darting. The call note is similar to that of Northern Rough-winged Swallow, but not quite as harsh. Bank Swallow forms large, premigratory flocks, often mixed with other swallow species, in late summer.

Cliff Swallow *Hirundo pyrrhonota* 5¹/₂ in. p.186

Common summer (April through Sept.) resident.

Visitors to the lakes around LBL should sing the praises

of this flying insect trap. Its sole diet is flying insects, and it takes not only mosquitoes, but other pests as well. The back, tail, and upper wing surfaces are dark brown to bluish-brown, contrasting with a buff-colored rump. The top of the head is blue-black with a light buff or rusty forehead patch. Chestnut on the throat extends well up onto each side of the neck. A whitish collar on the back of the neck fuses with the off-white underparts. The tail is either squared-off at its tip or only slightly notched. A recent invader of LBL, Cliff Swallow now occurs there during the summer months in large nesting colonies under several bridges. There they build their jug-shaped mud nests (see photograph), sometimes hundreds in a single colony. Colonies may be occupied for several years and then suddenly abandoned for one or a few years; this habit may be related to the buildup of dense populations of nest parasites (known as "swallow bugs," which may kill the vulnerable nestlings). The call note is a rather low, harsh "churr," the song a series of harsh, guttural twitters and squeaks.

Barn Swallow *Hirundo rustica* 6³/₄ in. p.186
Common summer (late March to early Oct.) resident.

The long, deeply forked tail of Barn Swallow is unique among the regularly occurring birds of LBL. Adult males are a deep, glossy blue above, with just a bit of white showing in the expanded tail. There is a chestnut patch on the forehead; the throat is also chestnut. Underparts (except the throat) are buff to cinnamon. Females and immatures resemble adult males but are duller. Barn Swallow feeds over open water and in a variety of terrestrial habitats. It may follow farm machinery or livestock, feeding on the flushed insects. Effortless, graceful fliers, they are a joy to watch as they forage on aerial insects, making pass after pass over favorite sites. A gregarious swallow, it nests in small colonies on porches, in outbuildings, and under bridges and culverts. The cup-shaped, grass-reinforced, mud nests are commonly attached to a vertical surface, such as a beam, rafter, or wall, often—coincidentally—near an Eastern Phoebe nest. The nest is lined with feathers and protected from dissolution during heavy rains by the "roof" overhead: Barn Swallow is thus one of many species whose natural histories have accommodated well the human modifications to their natural environment. Very vocal birds, the song is a rich mixture of notes—some clear, others harsh, gurgling, twittering, or guttural. They will defend their nests vigorously against menaces, diving repeatedly and closely at the intruder's head while uttering their alarm note, a loud "ee-tee," or "teet."

Blue Jay *Cyanocitta cristata* 11^1/$_2$ in.   **p.187**
Common permanent resident.

Unmistakable, this member of the family that includes crows is the only jay of LBL. This blue, black, gray, and white bird is named after its dominant color and one of its numerous calls. The upperparts are mostly blue, barred with black in the wings and tail. The prominent crest is blue, and there is a bold, black collar completely encircling the neck. The wings and corners of the tail show extensive white; the underparts are light gray. Blue Jay occurs in a wide variety of habitats in LBL, though usually not far from trees. It is an opportunistic feeder on many kinds of animals and plants: insects, seeds, berries, acorns, eggs, carrion, and small vertebrates (including nestling birds) are all taken as available. Among its many vocalizations are a scream (that sounds very much like a Red-shouldered Hawk); a clear, whistled, two-syllabled "pump-handle" call (sounds like a squeaking pump handle); and the harsh "jaay" namesake notes. May form loose flocks during the non-breeding season. The nest is placed in a tree crotch, on a horizontal limb, or in a thicket. It is bulky but well made, with a nice central cup lined with soft materials.

American Crow *Corvus brachyrhynchos* 18^1/$_2$ in. **p.187**
Common permanent resident.

This relative of jays, ravens, and magpies is black everywhere, though in strong sunlight there is a purplish—almost iridescent—hue to the feathers, especially those of the wings and back. Its flight is steady, with gliding episodes lasting only a few seconds (except, sometimes, when descending in altitude). If seen clearly it is unmistakable among the birds of LBL, although the very similar Fish Crow may be about to extend its summer range into LBL from the west. The voice of American Crow is a loud "caw," though juvenile birds have a softer, more nasal call. Often forms large roosting flocks during the winter months. Fond of mobbing owls and hawks, it may itself be the target of mobbing behavior by several species of song-birds. (The function of mobbing—a massed attack by smaller birds launched against a larger predatory bird—is not well understood. One suggested function, supported by some experimental evidence, is that mobbing provides a behavioral tool for transmitting information to young birds on who their local enemies are; in other words, a way of transmitting cultural traditions.) American Crow occurs in most habitats of LBL, but usually is found not far from trees. It has a varied diet of plant and animal material, and is an opportunistic scavenger and predator. Gregarious and intelligent, it is wary of humans in areas where it is hunted, but may become rather approachable in urban and residential areas where it is not persecuted. Sport hunting of crows usually involves the use of stuffed or dummy owls which the crows cannot resist approaching in order to harass.

Carolina Chickadee *Parus carolinensis* 4^1/$_2$ in. **p.188** Common permanent resident.

The only chickadee in LBL. The head is jet black from the lower margin of the eyes up; the throat is also black. These black areas are separated by a broad, triangular white patch on the side of the face. The back, wings, and tail are slate-gray, the breast white, and the belly, sides, and flanks buff. Wherever you find Tufted Titmouse in LBL you are also likely to find Carolina Chickadee; in winter these two species often form mixed loose flocks. Energetic, noisy birds, a common call is a nasal, "chick-a-dee-dee-dee." The spring song is a clear, whistled "vee-bee, vee-bay" the first note of each couplet higher-pitched, and the second couplet lower-pitched than the first. Rarely seen on or near the ground. Though it may excavate its own nest cavity in rotten wood, it usually uses old wood-pecker holes, natural cavities (or even unnatural ones—

I've known them to nest in vertical metal pipes supporting a clothesline), and nest boxes. Very similar to Black-capped Chickadee, which replaces Carolina Chickadee at higher latitudes and altitudes. Carolina Chickadee is smaller, shows less white on the wing, has a more sharply defined lower edge to the black throat patch, and has different vocalizations. In the few areas where these species occur together during breeding season, hybridization may occur. Eats insects, spiders, seeds, and some small berries (the berries of poison ivy are a favorite).

Tufted Titmouse *Parus bicolor* 5³/₄ in.   **p.188**
Common permanent resident.

One of the most characteristic birds of the forests of LBL, Tufted Titmouse—though it may not look it—is closely related to Carolina Chickadee. It is the only small, gray, tufted bird in the region. The solid gray upperparts contrast with much lighter underparts, accented with buff on the flanks. The face is light gray; adults have a black forehead patch. A common associate of Carolina Chickadee, they forage together for insects and seeds in the middle to upper layers of middle-aged to mature forests, and in semiopen areas. Tufted Titmouse is a hole nester and readily accepts bird boxes. Incubating birds are loathe to flush and will often stay on the nest even when the lid of the nest box is raised. The song is a series of loud, clear, two-syllabled whistles, something like "peter, peter, peter, peter." Various chickadee-like notes are also given. In late summer family groups may be found foraging through the forest together. In winter, loose, mixed-species feeding flocks of Tufted Titmouse, Carolina Chickadee, White-breasted Nuthatch, and Downy Woodpecker may form. Tufted Titmouse is a regular visitor to local bird feeders.

Red-breasted Nuthatch *Sitta canadensis* 4¹/₂ in.
Rare winter (Sept. to mid-May) resident.

A tiny bird, Red-breasted Nuthatch is fond of conifers. It resembles White-breasted Nuthatch, but is smaller, has rusty red underparts, and sports a conspicuous black stripe extending back from the base of the bill, through the eye, and down the side of the neck to the shoulder region (this black facial stripe is separated from the black crown by a white eyebrow line). The song is a higher-pitched, muted, tinny version of that of White-breasted Nuthatch. Diet is mainly conifer seeds, but some bark insects are included. An irregular migrant, Red-breasted Nuthatch fluctuates from year to year in its abundance at LBL; these fluctuations presumably reflect the availability of conifer seeds further north.

White-breasted Nuthatch *Sitta carolinensis* 5³/₄ in. **p.188**
Fairly common permanent resident.

The adult male is blue-gray above, except for a black cap and some white in the corners of the tail. The black cap extends down each side of the neck as a sort of half-collar. Underparts are white to light gray, except for a rusty wash on the belly. The bill is long, straight, and pointed. Females and immatures are similar to adult males, but have a deep bluish-gray cap. The white throat distinguishes White-breasted Nuthatch from the vaguely similar, but black-throated, Carolina Chickadee. Large feet and powerful leg muscles enable nuthatches to scurry over the bark of trunks and branches at any angle (it doesn't use its tail feathers as a prop as woodpeckers and Brown Creeper do) as it searches for insects in bark crevices. The name "upside-down-bird" is sometimes used for nuthatches because of their penchant for walking down vertical tree trunks headfirst. A cavity nester, it does not excavate its own nest but instead uses abandoned woodpecker holes or natural cavities. The song is a series of 5 to 15 whirry, monotone whistles, suggesting an automobile engine (a '48 Ford in my mind) that will crank but won't start. The characteristic call note is a loud, nasal "yank."

Brown Creeper *Certhia americana* 5¹/₄ in. **p.189**
Uncommon winter (mid-Sept. through April) resident.

This strange little bird looks a little like a wren and acts sort of like a woodpecker. It is well-adapted to its habit of "hitching" up tree trunks, woodpecker fashion, as it probes for spiders and insects in bark crevices with its long, thin, decurved bill. The central shafts of its long tail feathers are stiff and serve as a prop against the tree bark. Brown Creeper typically alights low on a tree trunk and then creeps upward, often in a spiral, until it is high up the tree; then it flies to the base of another tree and repeats the process. Its brown, buff-streaked upperparts make it inconspicuous against the bark. There is a whitish eyebrow stripe, underparts are a dingy white, and the rump is reddish. The song is a high-pitched, sibilant warble. More commonly heard in LBL than the song is its call note: a one- or two-syllabled, high-pitched, thin, lisping "zeep," or "zeet, zeet." Brown Creeper is an easily overlooked species, given its habits and appearance, and is more common than many people realize. When threatened, if may "hide" against the tree bark by flattening itself, spreading its wings and tail slightly, and remaining motionless. Usually builds its nest behind loose tree bark (see photograph).

Carolina Wren *Thryothorus ludovicianus* 5³/₄ in. p.189
Common permanent resident.

The most common and largest wren of LBL. Upperparts are brown to reddish-brown. Underparts are buff to cinnamon, except for a whitish throat. There is a distinct white eyebrow stripe, and the tail lacks white corners (present in Bewick's Wren). The tail, moderately long for a wren, is often held—wren-fashion—at a sharp angle to the body. Carolina Wren loves undergrowth in wooded or semiopen, preferably moist, environments. Commonly nests near, or even in, man-made structures (porches, outbuildings, mailboxes, etc.). An active, fairly tame bird. An accomplished songster, each male typically has a repertoire of many (two to three dozen) songs, apparently with favorites among them. Its voice is loud and clear, low-pitched, and carries well. A common song is a loud and ringing "kettle-tea, kettle-tea, kettle-tea, kett." Also frequently given is a loud "whittaker, whittaker, whittaker, whit." Some songs closely resemble some of Northern Cardinal and Kentucky Warbler. (After 30 years of listening to hundreds of renditions of the songs of each of these species every year, I'm still not always sure which one I'm hearing; maybe it's just me, or maybe there is some mimicking going on.) Carolina

Wren defends its territory year-round, and may sing at any season, and at any hour of the day. Besides a rich array of scolding notes, there is a common and distinctive down-slurred call note, lasting about a second, that is often given. Eats insects and other small invertebrates, and some seeds and berries (including poison ivy berries).

Bewick's Wren *Thryomanes bewickii* 5¹/₄ in.

Permanent resident; rare summer (April through Sept.), extremely rare winter.

Bewick's (pronounced "Buicks") Wren resembles Carolina Wren but is slightly smaller, is grayer above, has buff below much reduced and restricted mainly to flanks, and has white tail corners. This species has declined in numbers in LBL from fairly common to rare just since 1965. A checklist of birds of the Kentucky Woodlands National Wildlife Refuge (that refuge became part of LBL in 1964 when LBL was established), based on bird records from 1938 through 1956, listed Bewick's Wren as abundant. This decline is not just a local phenomenon; in recent decades this species has undergone a serious population decline in most of its range east of the Mississippi River. In the late 1980s however, several Bewick's Wrens, and at least one successful nest, were found in slash piles on clear cut areas of timberland in southern Stewart County, Tennessee. Timber harvest in LBL has involved some limited clear cuts, and more and larger ones are planned. Perhaps one incidental effect of such cutting will be to provide habitat for this delightful bird with its beautiful song. The song begins with 2 to 4 clear, whistled notes, on different pitches, followed by a long, quavering final note— the final note always higher-pitched than the penultimate note. Look, and listen, for Bewick's Wren in areas with few trees and with dense brush tangles. Diet includes insects and spiders.

House Wren *Troglodytes aedon* 4³/₄ in.

Extremely rare summer (April through Oct.) resident.

This jaunty, friendly, drab little wren, with its bubbly, gurgling song, is generally familiar to LBL visitors who have lived in more northern parts of the U.S. As suggested by its name, it seems to enjoy human proximity, and reaches some of its highest population densities in suburban areas of the northern U.S. Though it is a fairly common breeding bird in some cities in the vicinity, in LBL itself it is quite rare. Brownish-gray above; dingy below. A faint, buffy eyebrow stripe and eye-ring are visible at close range. The tail is short, lacks any white, and is usually held cocked up. A cavity or cranny nester, it readily takes to birdhouses. As is common in several wren species, the courting male may build one or a few "dummy" nests which are not used and usually not completely finished. During the breeding season males may sing incessantly from dawn to dusk. House Wren's diet includes various small invertebrates, but mainly insects.

Winter Wren *Troglodytes troglodytes* 4 in.
Uncommon winter (late Sept. to mid-April) resident.

Our smallest wren, with one of the most fantastic songs of any bird in LBL. It is dark, chocolate-brown above, with a faint buff eyebrow line and stubby, cocked tail. The underparts are dark and heavily barred on the belly and flanks, with a lighter breast and throat. Prefers streamsides, gullies, and lower slopes where there is dense undergrowth or root tangles. In such places it spends most of its time on or near the ground, teetering, hopping, darting, and flitting, mouselike, through the tangles in search of spiders and insects. The song is a long, bubbly cascade of high-pitched warbles and trills, lasting several seconds. The complexity of the song's structure can only be appreciated by the human ear on a slowed-down playback of the recorded song. A distinctive call note, heard much more frequently in winter than the song, is a one-or-two-syllabled "kip," or "kip, kip." It feeds on insects and spiders.

Sedge Wren *Cistothorus platensis* 4¼ in.
Uncommon spring (mid-April to late May) and fall (Aug. through Oct.) transient.

A small, light-colored wren that prefers wet, tall-grass meadows or sedgy marshes. The dominant color above is a warm, pale brown, with black and white streaks on the back and crown, and a buffy eyeline. The underparts are buff, with a yellowish wash on the sides and flanks. Both the tail and bill are short, even for a wren, giving the bird a juvenile look. Though furtive and difficult to see, this bird can usually be detected by its staccato song, which begins on a few to several sharp "chip" notes, then changes abruptly into a chattering, terminal trill. Sometimes sings at night. Feeds on insects and spiders.

Marsh Wren *Cistothorus palustris* 5 in.
Uncommon spring (mid-April to late May) and fall (Aug. through Oct.) transient.

A pretty wren with rusty brown upperparts, a black-and-white- striped patch on its back, and a prominent white eyebrow stripe. Underparts are dingy white with cinnamon flanks. Definitely a wren of wet marshes, it especially likes dense cattail and bulrush stands, where it hops from stem to stem as it forages for insects and snails. The song begins with one or two sharp, unmusical, grating notes, followed by a higher note, and that followed by a hurried, raspy warble or trill. During breeding season Marsh Wren may sing at any hour of the day or night.

Golden-crowned Kinglet *Regulus satrapa* 3³/₄ in.
Fairly common winter (late Sept. through April) resident.

This tiny (in LBL, only Ruby-throated Hummingbird is smaller, though Winter Wren is about the same size) lover of the forest canopy commonly flits its wings as it seeks insects, spiders, berries, seeds, and tree sap; it sometimes hovers as it examines or captures a morsel from a leaf or twig. The crown patch (golden in females, or orange-with-yellow-border in males) is not easily seen, given the small size and usually overhead position of the birds. The black and white facial stripes are normally discernible however, and they, plus the bird's small size and flitty behavior, are diagnostic. The upperparts are generally olive, and there are two white wing bars. Underparts are light gray. The song, so weak and high-pitched that humans seldom hear it, begins as a series of high, thin, wiry notes that tend to drop in pitch slightly and merge into a trill toward the end. The call notes—a series of three (usually) high, lisping notes, "zee, zee, zee,"—are more commonly heard than the song, and, once learned, are the easiest way to detect this species.

Ruby-crowned Kinglet *Regulus calendula* 4¹/₄ in.
Fairly common winter (mid-Sept. to mid-May) resident.

A little larger than Golden-crowned Kinglet, Ruby-crowned Kinglet behaves similarly and is found in similar habitats. From the head back, the two species are virtually identical in appearance. Ruby-crowned Kinglet lacks the black and white stripes on the face, having instead a conspicuous white eye-ring. The crown patch (absent in females) is ruby red, much smaller, not bordered by black, and often concealed. The song of Ruby-crowned Kinglet begins with two or three high, thin notes, followed by two or three lower-pitched notes, and ends in a sort of trill or warble. The call note is distinctive—a hurried "jee-dit," or "jee-dit, jee-dit."

Blue-gray Gnatcatcher *Polioptila caerulea* 4¹/₄ in.
p.190
Common summer (late March through Oct.) resident.

When you first spot this bird, you may think you are seeing a tiny mockingbird because shape and dominant colors are similar. Blue-gray Gnatcatcher is blue-gray above, light gray below. The legs and tail are long, the tail black above (except for white outer tail feathers), mostly white below, and often held cocked up. There is a thin white eye-ring in all plumages, and adult males (see photograph) have a black forehead that extends back over each eye as a black eyebrow stripe. The wings lack conspicuous white patches, but many wing feathers have whitish edges. Females and immatures are grayer than adult males. Blue-gray Gnatcatcher prefers wooded to semiopen conditions, including brushy edges. There it hawks for insects, which it may catch in midair, flycatcher-fashion. When perched it frequently flits its tail. The song is an easily overlooked, unimpressive series of thin, insectlike notes, followed by a weak warble. More commonly and easily heard is the call note, a high, buzzy "speee," repeated tirelessly. Prefers the middle to upper layers of the forest. The beautiful, cup-like nest is built astride a small branch; covered on the outside with bits of lichen and held together with spiderweb, the whole affair resembles a knot on the branch. Blue-gray Gnatcatcher eats insects and spiders.

Eastern Bluebird *Sialia sialis* 6³/₄ in.   **p.190**
Common permanent resident.

The adult male (see photograph) is unmistakable, with his deep blue upperparts, chestnut throat, breast, sides, and sides of neck, and white belly. Females are similar, but the chestnut is replaced by cinnamon-buff and the blue above is subdued and restricted mostly to the wings and tail (though a faint bluish wash is sometimes noticeable on the back and head). Juveniles just off the nest have a conspicuously spotted breast and back, and—like adult females—a light eye-ring. Bluebirds are thrushes (the spotted breasts of juveniles are a clue to that fact) and prefer semiopen areas where there is considerable open ground that can be scanned from convenient perches. When an insect is spotted, the bird swoops down upon it, usually retiring to a nearby perch to dine. Eastern Bluebird has a chunky, hunched appearance when perched, making it identifiable by silhouette alone from surprisingly long distances. In many areas Eastern Bluebird, a secondary cavity nester (meaning it does not excavate its own nest cavities), must compete—usually unsuccessfully—with the aggressive European Starling and House Sparrow, two exotic "weed" species. Prolonged, severe winter cold spells periodically decimate Eastern Bluebird populations in LBL. Ice storms, which make inaccessible the berries and fleshy fruits that are its major winter food, can also be disastrous. Its ability to raise three broods in a single good season allows it eventually to recover from severe population crashes. The song is a series of three or four soft, gurgling, warbled notes. A characteristic note is a melodious "tru-ly."

Veery *Catharus fuscescens* 7¹/₄ in.
Uncommon spring (mid-April to late May), rare fall (late Aug. to early Oct.) transient.

This, the drabbest of the seven species of thrushes that occur in LBL, is tawny above (including wings and tail), and, except for a faintly spotted, pale buff breast, mostly white below. A faint eye-ring may be visible. Veery loves heavily forested areas where it stays near or on the ground. The song is a credit to its family, and is the basis for the onomatopoeic common name. Flutelike, breezy, mellow, haunting, ethereal, liquid, vibrant, and wheeling are all words that have been used to describe Veery's song. While choice of adjectives may differ, the song is distinctive and—most would agree—beautiful. The series of notes, each of which is down-slurred (and shorter than the preceding) descends the pitch scale, while the tempo increases. Difficult to describe, but lovely to hear. Veery feeds on insects and berries.

Gray-cheeked Thrush *Catharus minimus* 7¹/₂ in.
Uncommon spring (early April to early June) and fall (early Sept. to late Oct.) transient.

This and the next species (Swainson's Thrush) look very much alike, but if seen well they can usually be reliably identified. Gray-cheeked Thrush is grayish-brown above (including wings and tail), whitish below. The breast is prominently spotted and does not usually show the buff wash that characterizes Veery and Swainson's Thrush. Gray-cheeked Thrush has a distinctly grayish cheek patch; sometimes a faint, grayish eye-ring is apparent. A retiring, shy bird, it occurs in brushy, wooded habitats, usually near ground level. The song resembles that of Veery, but is not as forceful, is slightly more nasal, and has a distinctive up-slurred terminal note. Diet includes insects, fruits, and berries.

Swainson's Thrush *Catharus ustulatus* 7 in.   p.191
Fairly common spring (mid-April to early June) and fall (Sept. through Oct.) transient.

One of five species of typical thrushes (Eastern Bluebird

99

and American Robin are thrushes, but are not typically plumaged for thrushes) found in LBL, Swainson's Thrush resembles Gray-cheeked most closely. The upperparts, including wings and tail, are solid grayish-brown as in Gray-cheeked Thrush (not as warm as in Veery). The underparts also resemble Gray-cheeked Thrush, except that there is a distinct buffish cast (indistinct in Gray-cheeked) to the upper breast extending onto the sides of the neck, the cheek, and noticeable on the face as an eye-ring or spectacles. The song of Swainson's Thrush is, in tonal quality, similar to that of Veery, but the pitch changes (both within individual notes and between successive notes) are reversed—rising rather than falling. Prefers wooded to semiopen country, often brushy, where it stays in the middle to lower levels of the vegetation. Eats insects and berries.

Hermit Thrush *Catharus guttatus* 7 in.
Uncommon winter (late Sept. to early May) resident.

Except for American Robin and Eastern Bluebird, Hermit Thrush is the only thrush species found in LBL in the dead of winter. It prefers moist—even marshy—areas, like those around beaver ponds and in wooded ravines. The reddish tail, contrasting with an olive-brown back, distinguishes it from all other thrushes in LBL. (Fox Sparrow also has a reddish tail, but shows much rust on its wings, breast, and back as well. Further, it has a conical bill instead of the longer, thinner bill typical of thrushes.) Otherwise it looks much like Swainson's or Gray-cheeked thrushes. Hermit Thrush has a peculiar habit of cocking its tail up at an angle and then slowly lowering it to normal position while standing. It feeds, usually near ground level, on invertebrates, occasional small vertebrates such as salamanders, and berries. The song of three or four phrases—the opening note of each phrase prolonged, and each phrase on a different pitch—has a flutelike quality. In LBL however, the bird rarely sings, but commonly gives its distinctive "chuck" or "chuck-chuck" note.

Wood Thrush *Hylocichla mustelina* 8 in.   **p.191**
Common summer (early April through Oct.) resident.

Except for American Robin, this is the largest thrush in LBL, and the only typical thrush (Eastern Bluebird and American Robin are both, in terms of their plumage patterns, atypical thrushes) to nest there. Wood Thrush is heavily spotted on breast, belly, and sides with large, round, bold black spots on a white background. Upperparts are brown or olive-brown on the tail, wings, rump, and lower back, becoming progressively more rufous from tail to head. The cheek is gray streaked with white, and there is a light eye-ring. Wood Thrush occurs in mature deciduous woodlands, especially near water, on moist lower slopes and in wooded ravines. The song, one of the most beautiful and characteristic sounds of summer in the forests of LBL, is a series of varied, clear, flutelike phrases, often including a distinctive "we-o-leee" (the last note trilled and drawn out). When alarmed, may utter a rapid, scolding "pip,pip,pip." A low, liquid "quoit" may be given near the nest. Diet consists largely of insects, spiders, and fruits.

American Robin *Turdus migratorius* 10 in.   **p.192**
Common permanent resident.

Our largest thrush. Adult male (see photograph) is dark, grayish-brown above, shading to black on the head and tail. The throat is black and white striped, and there is a broken white eye-ring. Behind the throat the underparts are brick red, except for white on the posterior belly and undertail coverts. The bill is yellow (darkish toward its tip), and some white shows at the corners of the tail. Adult females resemble males but have gray rather than black heads, dark gray rather than yellow bills, are brown above, and paler russet on the underparts. Juvenile birds are heavily spotted beneath (like adults of typical thrushes); though they lack the extensive rufous of the adults, they are washed with cinnamon-buff beneath. A habitat generalist, American Robin breeds in wooded or semiopen areas where the cup-like nest, constructed of mud reinforced with plant materials, is placed on a low platform or lodged in the fork of a branch. In winter they commonly form large flocks which often congregate along waterways and in moist bottomlands. Earthworms, located by keen eyesight, are a favorite food. This fondness for earthworms, which in turn may have fed on contaminated leaves, makes American Robin especially susceptible to the effects of insecticide spraying. It also feeds on insects and berries. The song is a series of loud, clear, short phrases, varying only slightly and inconsistently in pitch.

Gray Catbird *Dumetella carolinensis* 8³/₄ in. p.192
Fairly common summer (April through Oct.) resident.
This slate-gray bird, with a black cap and chestnut undertail coverts, is a skulker, fond of dense, low vegetation in the form of thickets and vine tangles; it rarely ventures far from such cover. The tail, which may be nearly as black as the bird's cap, is moderately long, but not as proportionately long as in the other two mimic thrushes which occur in LBL (Northern Mockingbird and Brown Thrasher). Gray Catbird is usually seen (but more often only heard) near the ground, though breeding males often choose loftier, more conspicuous singing perches. Named because of a distinctive "mewing" note that it utters, its song is an unmelodic series of diverse notes—some musical, some harsh, some growling, some squawky—but individual notes aren't immediately repeated. The overall effect is quite cacophonous. Gray Catbird is not as given to or as good at mimicking sounds it hears in its environment as are Northern Mockingbird and Brown Thrasher. Insects, spiders, and berries are dietary staples.

Northern Mockingbird *Mimus polyglottos* 10¹/₂ in. **p.193**
Common permanent resident.
The official state bird of Tennessee—and several other states as well—Northern Mockingbird is gray above, white below, shows extensive white in its wings and along the borders of its long tail, and has a slender, pointed bill. The "Northern" in its name simply means that, of the North American species of mockingbirds, this is the one which occurs farthest north; in the U.S. it is quite properly thought of as a bird of the South, though in recent

decades it has been extending its range northward. Northern Mockingbird is fairly beloved by most everyone. I say "fairly" beloved because it does have a couple of traits which disendear it to some people: unmated males may sing at all hours of the night when you're trying to sleep, and it may harass other species at bird feeders, though it only rarely eats there itself. The song, which may begin on the wing, is loud and varied. Typically it is a long series of phrases, each phrase repeated several times before the bird switches—without pause—to a completely different phrase, which it repeats several times, etc. It is an excellent mimic, imitating not only the songs and calls of several other local birds, but sometimes even the sounds of machines that it hears regularly. Found in a variety of open or semiopen habitats, including urban areas. When seeking insects or confronting predators, Northern Mockingbird may flash its white wing patches conspicuously, probably to startle the insects into movement, and to confuse and intimidate predators. Northern Mockingbird feeds on insects and other invertebrates, small vertebrates, and berries.

Brown Thrasher *Toxostoma rufum* 11½ in. **p.193**
Permanent resident. Common summer (March through Nov.), uncommon winter (Dec. through Feb.).

This long-tailed, rufous, mimic thrush is the largest member of its family in LBL. Sometimes called "brown thrush," it is not a true thrush, though its plumage certainly suggests a thrush. Rufous dominates above, but is relieved by two white wing bars and a grayish-buff face. The underparts are cream, punctuated with several rows of bold, chocolate-brown, elongated spots on the breast, sides, and belly. The bill is long, pointed, and slightly downcurved. Though most Brown Thrashers leave LBL in winter for warmer climes, some may be found there year-round. No one knows if winter residents are the same individuals that breed in LBL in the summer, or if they are different individuals who have nested farther north and come to LBL to pass the relatively mild winter. Brown Thrasher prefers thickets, dense undergrowth, briar and vine tangles, fencerows, and woodland edges. It is a bit secretive, although singing males habitually choose conspicuous perches for their performances. The song is similar to that of Northern Mockingbird, but with each phrase repeated only once (i.e., uttered twice) instead of several times. It feeds on invertebrates, small vertebrates, and fruits; food items hidden beneath ground litter are sometimes exposed by using the strong bill as a rake.

American Pipit *Anthus rubescens* 6¹/₂ in.
Uncommon winter (late Sept. to early May) resident.

A bird of open country, especially mowed grasslands, freshly sown agricultural fields, and even plowed ground. It is slimmer and longer-tailed than most sparrows, has a finer bill, and walks rather than hops. Seldom perches far from the ground. Continually bobs its tail. Upperparts are brownish-gray; underparts are light tan to flesh-colored. Back, sides, and breast are lightly streaked with brown. Sports a buffy eyebrow stripe and two buff wing bars. Tail is mostly blackish, but with white outer feathers. Fall and winter birds similar, but darker above, more boldly streaked and with less pink below. Look for flocks of these birds in their preferred habitat (see above), and on lakeside beaches and mudflats. The most commonly heard vocalization of this species in LBL is a high-pitched, 1-to-4-syllabled call note (often given in flight) from which it gets its common name: "pit," "pip-it," or "peeet," etc. Pipits blend in well with their surroundings and are easily overlooked unless they flush and show their white outer tail feathers in flight. They are often detected as they fly overhead, uttering their characteristic call note.

Cedar Waxwing *Bombycilla cedrorum* 7¹/₄ in.   p.194
Permanent resident. Fairly common winter (Oct. through May), rare summer (June through Sept). Abundance fluctuates from year to year.

As "penguin" suggests "formal," so "waxwing" suggests "elegant." Elegant indeed—and sleek. The warm brown of the bird's back, head, and breast contrasts with the gray of the wings, rump, and tail. The face sports a coal-black, white-edged mask that extends back to the base of a

104

prominent crest. The belly and lower breast are yellowish; the undertail coverts are white. The throat and bill are black, and there is a sulfur-yellow band at the tip of the tail. The tips of the secondary feathers of the adult bird's (see photograph) wings bear brilliant red spots which suggest sealing wax, hence the common name. Young birds are grayer, and faintly streaked below. During the non-breeding season Cedar Waxwings form tight flocks that move from tree to tree or bush to bush, usually in open or semiopen habitats, in search of their favorite food—berries (of many kinds). Land Between The Lakes is near the southern edge of the breeding range of this species, but nests have been found at Piney Campground in southwest LBL, and at the visitor's center at Golden Pond. Cedar Waxwing is quite vocal, but the call is easily overlooked—until you learn it, that is—and then it's amazing how often you hear it. The notes are thin, high-pitched, monotone, and sibilant in the extreme—sometimes with a slight quaver. People who grow old watching—and listening to—birds can estimate crudely their rate of hearing loss with the passing years by noting which bird calls they can no longer hear; higher-frequency sounds are usually the first to go, and if the notes of Cedar Waxwing are still audible, the person's hearing is probably still pretty good; if Pileated Woodpecker's cannot be heard, it's probably time to visit your ear doctor.

Loggerhead Shrike *Lanius ludovicianus* 9 in.　　**p.194**
Uncommon permanent resident.

Though a true songbird, Loggerhead Shrike acts like a hawk. It is gray, black, and white, suggesting at first glance Northern Mockingbird. The back, rump, nape, and top of head are pearl gray. The wings and tail are predominantly black, with considerable white showing in flight. A stout, hooked, black bill, which at its base meets a broad, black mask extending back through the eye to the ear region gives the bird a bandit-like appearance. The underparts are light gray. The song, rarely heard, is a series of soft warbles and harsh squeaks, each phrase likely to be repeated; it is suggestive of Brown Thrasher's song, but more subdued. Loggerhead Shrike preys on insects and small vertebrates, which it captures in open areas that provide scattered trees or other lookout perches. Its habit of impaling its prey on thorns or barbed wire has earned it the name of "butcher bird." Pesticides and habitat loss may be responsible for the severe decline in Loggerhead Shrike populations in the central and eastern U.S. in recent decades.

European Starling *Sturnus vulgaris* 8^1/$_4$ in.   **p.195**
Common permanent resident.

This member of the Old World family that includes the myna birds of the pet trade was introduced into this country during the last century. Since that introduction it has been, from its own perspective at least, one of the super success stories among North American birds, having expanded its range to include all of the continental U.S. (except Alaska), most of Mexico, and much of Canada. It is a noxious weed among birds, competing with many native species for food and nesting sites. It looks like a stout, short-tailed blackbird, and during the nonbreeding season commonly forms flocks—sometimes in spectacular numbers—with several native species of blackbirds. Spring birds (see photograph) are an iridescent, greenish-purplish black with a bright yellow bill. Immature birds are solid dusky brown. Fall birds are heavily speckled with buff, but these specks gradually disappear through the winter as the feather tips on which they are borne wear away. The bill is dark in nonbreeding birds. The ultimate habitat generalist among birds, European Starling is omnivorous and quite opportunistic in its feeding habits. It tends to range much farther from human habitations than does House Sparrow, another Old World species that was introduced into the U.S. last century. The usual sounds uttered by European Starling (I cannot make myself call them songs) are varied, harsh, guttural, metallic, and squeaky; it could do better I suspect, judging from the excellence with which it mimics calls of several native bird species.

White-eyed Vireo *Vireo griseus* 5 in.   **p.195**
Common summer (early April to mid-Oct.) resident.

The six vireos of LBL resemble warblers, but their bills

are heavier, slightly downcurved, and have a faint hook at their tips (warbler bills tend to be thin and needle-like). Be haviorally, vireos are less energetic, i.e. don't hop about as much as warblers. These differences between the two groups are usually of little help to beginning birders who haven't looked at that many warblers or vireos closely. But though the differences are slight, they are real, and practice and experience make them meaningful surprisingly quickly. Trust me. The namesake feature of White-eyed Vireo is unique among LBL vireos, but you must be looking at an adult bird (see photograph) at close range in order to see it. Upperparts are olive-gray; sides and flanks are pale yellowish, the underparts otherwise white (except that some individuals have a yellowish band across the upper breast). There are yellow spectacles on the face, and two whitish bars on each wing. Immatures resemble adults, but have dark irises. White-eyed Vireo loves thickets, typically in clearings, along woodland edges, along fencerows, or in overgrown fields. There it builds its beautiful cup nest, suspended from the fork of a branch. It sings a lot and loudly. The first and last notes (of the typical series of five to seven) are emphatic and distinctive "check" notes; the intervening notes are slurred, run together, and vary in pitch. Something like "check, chup-er-ee-o, check," though there is considerable variation from song to song, even in one individual's repertoire. It eats mostly insects, and some berries late in the season.

Solitary Vireo *Vireo solitarius* 5¹/₂ in.

Rare spring (early April to late May) and fall (Sept. through Oct.) transient.

A slate-gray head, white spectacles, two light wing bars, and yellowish sides and flanks on otherwise white underparts distinguish Solitary Vireo. It is a deliberate bird, and rather tame. The middle to upper levels of woodland vegetation are its preferred habitat. The song is robin-like—a short series of slurred notes resembling the song of Red-eyed Vireo but higher-pitched and less urgent, with longer pauses between songs. Diet mainly insects.

Yellow-throated Vireo *Vireo flavifrons* 5¹/₂ in.
Fairly common summer (early April to mid-Oct.) resident.

Bright yellow unstreaked throat and breast, yellow spectacles, two white wing bars, and a vireo (see account of White-eyed Vireo) bill serve to identify Yellow-throated Vireo. The upperparts are olive except for a gray rump. The belly, flanks, and undertail coverts are white. Mature, rather open woodlands, in the middle to upper levels of vegetation, are the usual haunts of this species. Its song sounds much like that of Red-eyed Vireo (which frequents the same habitats), but the individual notes of Yellow-throated Vireo's song have a distinctly raspy or burry quality, and the tempo is less urgent with slightly longer pauses between songs. It's primarily insectivorous, but eats some berries.

Warbling Vireo *Vireo gilvus* 5¹/₂ in.   **p.196**
Fairly common summer (early April through Sept.) resident.

The plainest of our vireos, and one of the most difficult to see well because of its preference for the uppermost branches of tall trees. Warbling Vireo is mostly gray, darker above and much lighter below. The gray of the crown contrasts with a light eyebrow stripe. There are no wing bars. It prefers tall trees in or adjacent to open areas (such as lake and stream margins), and parklike habitats near buildings, picnic areas, and camp grounds. Though it can be locally rather common, that fact is not likely to be appreciated until you learn to recognize its long, bubbly, unvireo-like song (which usually lasts about two seconds and consists of many notes, on various pitches, all run together into a warble). Primarily insectivorous.

Philadelphia Vireo *Vireo philadelphicus* 5 in.
Rare spring (mid-April to late May) and fall (early Sept. to mid-Oct.) transient.

The yellow breast and absence of wing bars distinguish this species from all other LBL vireos. Except for the yellowish breast and dark lores, it resembles Warbling Vireo. It is not as restricted in its foraging to the upper canopy as

Warbling Vireo. The song of Philadelphia Vireo is very similar to that of Red-eyed Vireo, but is slightly higher-pitched and slower. Diet mostly of insects, but a few berries included.

Red-eyed Vireo *Vireo olivaceus* 6 in.   **p.196**
Common summer (early April to mid-Oct.) resident.

A good candidate for the title "summer voice of the forests of LBL" (though surely not the only good candidate—Wood Thrush, for one, would make the contest interesting). The underparts are essentially white. The upperparts are olive-gray, with wings and tail slightly darker. The head is distinctive among the vireos of LBL, with its blue-gray cap, white eyebrow stripe, dark eyeline, and red iris (see photograph; iris brown in immatures). It lives in a variety of wooded habitats, from the interior of fairly dense, mature deciduous woodlands (on either lower, or drier upland, sites), to rather open parklike and residential areas. It prefers the middle layers of the forest vegetation, where it is ubiquitous but difficult to see. The song is ceaselessly uttered during the spring and summer, from dawn to dusk. Suggesting American Robin's song, the series of 1- to 3-noted phrases are more distinctly separated by by pauses. The individual notes lack the burry or raspy quality typical of Yellow-throated Vireo's song. Diet in LBL is almost exclusively insects.

Blue-winged Warbler *Vermivora pinus* 4¹/₂ in.
Summer resident. Uncommon spring (mid-April to mid-May), rare summer and fall (mid-May to mid-Sept.).

Warblers (i.e. New World warblers—Old World warblers are a different group) have been called the butterflies of the bird world. Parochially at least, the metaphor seems appropriate. As a group they are small, colorful, active, and insectivorous. Their straight, fine, needle-like bills serve well as forceps for catching small insects and spiders, the dietary staples of most species most of the time. Identifying them in the fall, after they have molted out of their breeding finery, can be very difficult—and rewarding. Don't try it without a good field guide and a passel of patience. Blue-winged Warbler has light olive upperparts, except for bluish-gray wings with two prominent, white wing bars. Underparts yellow, except for white undertail coverts. Face yellow, with a black streak extending from base of bill back through eye. Sexes similar, but yellow is paler in females. Prefers semiopen conditions of tall brush or small trees interspersed with lower vegetation; overgrown pastures and abandoned fields, as well as woodland borders and openings, are likely haunts. Males often sing from the topmost perches in small trees. Their most typical song is a two-syllabled "see-gee," the second syllable lower in pitch, and both syllables rather buzzy. Rarely, it sings a song indistinguishable (to my ears at least) from that of Field Sparrow. Blue-winged Warbler nests in clumps of vegetation on or very near the ground. It is a noticeably more common breeder just a few tens of miles to the east of LBL.

Golden-winged Warbler *Vermivora chrysoptera* 5 in. **p.197**
Uncommon spring (mid-April to mid-May), rare fall (Sept.) transient.

Upperparts mostly solid gray, underparts (except throat) whitish. Conspicuous yellow wing patch. Both sexes with dark (black in male, gray in female) throat and ear patches, and yellow foreheads (extending well back onto crown of male—see photograph). Song begins like that of Blue-winged Warbler, but ends on two to four low-pitched buzzy notes (instead of one, as in Blue-winged): "see, gee-gee-gee." Golden-winged Warbler prefers disturbed habitats in forested areas that harbor dense brush and weeds; abandoned fields, overgrown pastures, tree fall gaps, and tangled woodland edges are favored. Sometimes interbreeds with Blue-winged Warbler, resulting in intermediate hybrids such as the rare Brewster's Warbler and the extremely rare Lawrence's Warbler. Like all of our warblers, Golden-winged Warbler is primarily insectivorous.

Tennessee Warbler *Vermivora peregrina* 4-3/4 in.
Common spring (mid-April to mid-May), fairly common fall (Sept. through Oct.) transient.

The plumage of Tennessee Warbler suggests that of a vireo, but the needle-like bill and active habits mark it unmistakably as a warbler. Upperparts are greenish-olive. Underparts are whitish, with a gray or brown wash sometimes detectable on the sides. The female has a distinct yellowish wash on the breast. Breeding males have a gray crown and forehead, white eyebrow stripe, and faint eyeline. In females the top of the head is similar to the back in color, and the eyebrow stripe is yellowish. The song of Tennessee Warbler is variable, but always loud, vigorous, and—during spring migration—incessantly offered. A common version is "ti-zip, ti-zip, tsee-tsee-tsee-tsee-tsee." The song of Nashville Warbler is similar, but delivered with less urgency, and tending to fade at the end. Tennessee Warbler is a bird of the treetops during spring migration, but may be found feeding (only rarely singing) at many levels in wooded habitats in the fall. It prefers semiopen or brushy areas, and tends to avoid deep woodland interiors.

Orange-crowned Warbler *Vermivora celata* 5 in.
Rare spring (mid-April to mid-May) and fall (Oct.) transient; extremely rare winter resident.

A plain bird, Orange-crowned Warbler is olive above and has yellowish-green underparts with faint breast streaks. The namesake feature is difficult to see in the field. No wing bars or tail spots. Faint eyeline interrupts a yellowish eye-ring. Undertail coverts yellow (white in Tennessee Warbler). A weak songster, its trill suggests that of Pine Warbler and Chipping Sparrow, but sometimes varies in pitch and tends to fade toward the end. Brushy, overgrown (often densely) hillsides, thickets, and woodland borders are preferred habitat, usually low in the vegetation. An inconspicuous species, it may be more common than records suggest. Its fall migration peak is unusually late for transient warblers in LBL.

Nashville Warbler *Vermivora ruficapilla* 4³/₄ in.
Fairly common spring (mid-April to mid-May) and fall (Sept. to mid-Oct.) transient.

Upperparts olive-green, except grayer on head, especially in males. Conspicuous white eye-ring. No wing bars. Underparts (including throat) immaculate yellow, though sometimes there is white on flanks and lower belly. The chestnut-red crown patch of males is difficult to see in the field. The usual song resembles that of Tennessee Warbler, but is noticeably softer and less emphatic ("zee-wit, zee-wit, zee-wit, tee,tee, tee, tee, tee, tee, tee"), the terminal trill suggesting a Chipping Sparrow. Nashville Warbler feeds from near ground level to treetops, in brushy, overgrown areas and open woodlands.

Northern Parula *Parula americana* 4¹/₂ in.   p.197
Summer resident. Fairly common spring (early April to mid-May), uncommon summer and fall (mid-May to early Oct.).

Upperparts grayish-blue, except for a large, greenish "back patch." Two prominent white wing bars. White eye-ring is narrow and broken by a dark eyeline. Throat and breast yellow, belly and undertail coverts white. Broad, burnt orange band across breast prominent in male, much less prominent or even absent in females (see photograph), immatures, and fall males. The usual song is a buzzy trill, ascending in pitch and ending abruptly, the terminal note often slightly lower in pitch ("zzzzzzzzz-ip"). Less commonly it sings a song very similar to that of Cerulean Warbler. Northern Parula haunts the middle and upper reaches of mature trees along streams, lake margins, and swamps. Nests are variable in details of construction and nature of materials used (at least in LBL, where Spanish moss and old-man's-beard lichen—the nesting materials of choice—are not available), placed either low or high in a tree, well out on a horizontal limb; the nests are often pendant (suggesting the structure of Northern Oriole's nest), with opening to nest cavity on either the side or top of the structure.

Yellow Warbler *Dendroica petechia* 5 in.   p.198
Summer resident. Fairly common spring (early April to mid-May), uncommon summer and fall (mid-May to mid-Sept.).

Yellow indeed, more so than any other LBL warbler. Even the wing markings and tail spots are yellow, contrasting with the greenish wash of the upperparts. The black eyes look beadlike, set as they are in the all-yellow head. In immatures and females the yellowness may be quite muted, resulting in a dusky look, but even then the distinctive tail spots persist. Adult males (see photograph) have distinct, fine, rusty breast streaks (some females show traces of these). The song is a cheerful series of half-a-dozen or so high-pitched notes, dropping in pitch near the end, and sometimes with the very last note rising again ("see,see,see,see,teet,teet;" or, "see, see, see, see, teet, teet, peet"). Yellow Warbler prefers open, brushy areas, often near water. Lawns, gardens, orchards, and willow thickets around ponds are favored sites. The nest is built in a fork of a shrub or small tree, 2 to 12 feet up. A common victim of Brown-headed Cowbird nest parasitism, it sometimes defends itself by building a new floor to its nest, thereby entombing the parasite's eggs (and often some of its own) in the "basement." Up to six such "stories" have been found in a single nest, each with entombed eggs.

Chestnut-sided Warbler *Dendroica pensylvanica* 5 in.

p.198

Uncommon spring (mid-April to mid-May) and fall (Sept. to mid-Oct.) transient.

Spring adults are distinctive, with a chestnut streak on each side continuing onto the sides of the neck and lower face to a black spot at the base of the bill (this streak becomes black on the face in males), and a yellow (male) or greenish-yellow (female—see photograph) crown. Back boldly streaked with black; two whitish (pale yellow in females) wing bars. Underparts (except for chestnut streak described above) and ear region of face are white. Black eyeline present, bolder in male. Adults in the fall lose the black facial markings. Immatures lack the chestnut stripe, black on face, and yellow crown, but have the yellowish wing bars, whitish underparts, and a narrow white eye-ring. The song is similar to Yellow Warbler's, but the endings are different: in Chestnut-sided the penultimate note is typically higher-pitched than the opening series, and the terminal note drops in pitch (see,see,see,da-cree-chur). Chestnut-sided Warbler occurs in a wide variety of wooded or partially wooded habitats, as long as there is a brushy element involved.

Magnolia Warbler *Dendroica magnolia* 4³/₄ in.
Uncommon spring (mid-April to late May), fairly common fall (Sept. to mid-Oct.) transient.

Breeding birds are gray to blackish above, with yellow rump patch, white patches at mid-tail, and white wing patch (male) or wing bars (female). Underparts mostly bright yellow, with bold black stripes on sides and breast. Undertail coverts and underside of tail white, except for a broad black band across tail tip. Face black (dark gray in female) with white eyebrow stripe (gray in female). Immatures, and adults in fall, are browner above, and have a greenish-olive cast on the back; the eyebrow stripe is fainter; underparts are without conspicuous streaking (faint streaks often show along the sides); and a grayish breast band is usually evident in immatures. The song of Magnolia Warbler resembles that of Yellow Warbler, but is shorter and softer. To some it suggests Hooded Warbler's song. Look for Magnolia Warbler in wooded environments, of various types, at lower to middle layers of the vegetation.

Cape May Warbler *Dendroica tigrina* 5 in.
Rare spring (mid-April to mid-May) and fall (mid-Sept. to mid-Oct.) transient.

Noticeably more common in some years than in others. Chestnut cheek patches of breeding males are distinctive. A dark eyeline surmounts each cheek patch, and above the eyeline is a yellow eyebrow stripe; the eyebrow stripes are connected by a narrow yellow line on the lower forehead. Females lack the chestnut cheek patch, but have a yellow patch on each side of the neck (present also in males). Below, both sexes are yellow streaked with black, and have yellow rumps. Upperparts are mostly olive. Male has a black or blackish cap, black streaks on the back, and a white wing patch (female has two thin, white wing bars). Fall birds have streaked breasts, a greenish-yellow rump, white lower belly and undertail coverts, and often show a pale spot on each side of neck. Song is a series of 6 to 12 high-pitched, weak, buzzy notes, all on the same pitch. Look for Cape May Warbler in wooded areas, especially if the trees are widely spaced. There it feeds, often in small, loose flocks, at middle levels or in the lower

114

canopy. Cemeteries and treed lawns are frequented.

Black-throated Blue Warbler *Dendroica caerulescens*
5¹/₄ in.

Rare spring (mid-April to mid-May) and fall (mid-Sept. to mid-Oct.) transient.

The breeding male is elegant, even formal, with his blue or blue-gray upper parts, black face, throat, and sides, and pure white breast, belly, and undertail coverts. The wing has a conspicuous white spot near its outer margin (at the base of the primaries). Females are brownish-olive above, have a dark face, light eyebrow stripe, unstreaked yellowish-olive underparts, and a smaller white wing spot (typically smaller than in breeding males). The wing and tail feathers of females often have a distinct bluish cast. Song of Black-throated Blue Warbler is a slow, deliberate series of four or five buzzy notes, the last distinctly higher pitched: "zoo, zoo, zoo, zoo, zeeee." Prefers fairly mature deciduous woods, in understory to lower canopy layers.

Yellow-rumped Warbler *Dendroica coronata* 5¹/₂ in. p.199
Winter resident. Common spring (April to mid-May) and fall (late Sept. to late Nov.); uncommon winter.

The only species of warbler likely to be seen in LBL during the winter months (photograph is of a winter adult), though there are a few winter records of a few other warbler species. Adults show four yellow spots: the crown, the rump, and in front of each wing (immatures have only the yellow rump). Spring males are blue-gray above (excepting yellow patches as noted above), with streaked backs, two white wing bars, black face mask, white throat, thin white eyebrow stripe, black breast band, black-streaked sides, and white belly and undertail coverts. Adult female is similar to male, but has brown above where the male has gray, and has dark gray instead of black on the face, breast, and sides. All plumages show white spots in the spread tail. The song is a warble, or trill, rather weak and colorless, suggesting the song of Dark-eyed Junco. In LBL the note—a sharp "check"—is heard more often than the song. Look for Yellow-rumped Warbler in almost any terrestrial habitat in LBL, from mature woodlands to open fields, from ridgetop to lakeside. They eat mostly soft-bodied fruits (such as those of eastern red cedar, sumac, etc.) in cold weather when insects are not available; where concentrations of food occur, loose flocks of several to several dozen individuals may be encountered. The name "Myrtle Warbler" is still legitimately applied to the subspecies (race) of Yellow-rumped Warbler that occurs in the northern and eastern U.S., including LBL.

Black-throated Green Warbler *Dendroica virens* 4³/₄ in.
p.199

Fairly common spring (April to late May), uncommon fall (mid-Aug. through Oct.) transient.

All plumages have a yellow face and side of neck, interrupted by a greenish-gray ear patch (more distinct in immatures); there is a yellow eyebrow stripe. Breeding males (see photograph) have a solid black throat and breast; black on the sides is solid and continuous with the black breast in front, but breaks into blackish streaks behind. The crown, back, and rump are greenish-olive. There are two white wing bars. Belly and undertail coverts are white (except for a yellowish tinge on the flanks). Adult females similar to males, but with yellow (instead of black) throat. Immatures lack both the black throat and black breast. Song is five or six buzzy notes, the first few at one pitch, then one (sometimes two) at a distinctly lower pitch, and finally the last note given on the same pitch as the first notes: "see, see, see, see, su-zy." Black-throated Green Warbler occurs in woodlands and, less commonly, in overgrown, abandoned fields, where it feeds from middle to uppermost levels of the vegetation.

Blackburnian Warbler *Dendroica fusca* 5 in.

Uncommon spring (mid-April to late May), rare fall (late Aug. to early Oct.) transient.

The only warbler in LBL with a fiery-orange throat. Breeding males are predominantly black and white, except for intense orange on the throat and upper breast, and paler orange on the eyebrow stripe, top of head, and side of neck.

Lower breast, belly, and undertail coverts are whitish. Sides are streaked with black, there is a white wing patch, and white in the outer tail feathers. Face, nape, and periphery of crown are black. Female and immature birds are similar, but the orange of the breeding male is replaced with yellow, there is brown or gray where the breeding male has black, and there are two white wing bars instead of a single white wing patch. The song is variable, but is often a series of thin, high-pitched notes that tend to quicken in pace and rise in pitch, seeming to (or actually, depending on one's hearing) fade into inaudibly high frequencies. Blackburnian Warbler is always a bit of a shock to me when I first spy it, usually high in the branches of a tree, flitting about like some tiny, animated, incendiary device. It is rather catholic in its choice of habitats during migration, so long as there are some trees involved.

Yellow-throated Warbler *Dendroica dominica* 5¼ in.
Fairly common summer (late March to early Oct.) resident.

Both sexes have a bright yellow throat and upper breast, a white belly, black-streaked sides, gray upperparts, two white wing bars, a white patch on each side of the face behind the cheek, a white eyebrow stripe, and a black face patch which extends down onto the side of the neck. Medium-sized to large trees along waterways are the usual haunts of this beautiful songster. In LBL it is especially fond of sycamore trees. A persistent singer, it may be more difficult to see than to hear as it forages in the middle to uppermost reaches of the trees. Yellow-throated Warbler is, at least some of the time, a bark gleaner—diligently searching for insects and spiders in the crevices of the bark on the trunks and branches of trees. The song is a series of six or seven loud, clear notes that become more and more run-together and lower-pitched as the song progresses, with the last rising in pitch. Do not confuse the name of this warbler with those similarly named—but very different—species, Yellow-throated Vireo or Common Yellowthroat.

Pine Warbler *Dendroica pinus* 5¼ in.

Permanent resident. Fairly common summer (late March to early Oct.), rare winter.

Breeding male has a yellow throat and breast, an unstreaked olive back, and two white wing bars. Sides faintly streaked, belly and undertail coverts white. Females, fall males, and immatures similar to breeding male, but more subdued (especially the immatures)—with less yellow on underparts, and dingier wing bars. Aptly named, Pine Warbler is likely to be encountered in LBL anywhere there are pines. It feeds from the ground to the tops of the pines, often rather deliberately patrolling the branches and trunks in search of insects. Compared to other warblers its movements are rather sluggish. The song is weak but musical—resembling a languid version of Chipping Sparrow's vigorous monotone trill. Though the nest is always built in a pine, outside the breeding season Pine Warblers are less restricted to pine trees.

Prairie Warbler *Dendroica discolor* 4¾ in. **p.200**

Common summer (early April to late Sept.) resident.

Breeding male (see photograph) and female are similar in appearance (though the female is a bit paler), except that the male has several rows of chestnut spots on his back (rarely visible in the field, however). Throat, breast, and belly are yellow, upperparts are olive. Sides are streaked with black; has two yellowish wing bars. Face yellow, with two black streaks bounding a yellow patch beneath the eye. White spots in the tail are best seen as the bird flies. Immatures have more gray and less yellow on the head. A small warbler of brushy, abandoned fields with numerous saplings, often in dry, upland areas. It is not—as its name suggests—a bird of prairies or grasslands. A good field mark is its habit of tail-bobbing while perched. The song is a series of five to a dozen or more buzzy, usually distinct notes that ascend the scale. Suggests the song of Northern Parula, except that in that species there are typically no individually discernible notes. Though it generally forages in the middle to lower layers of the vegetation, singing males are fond of the topmost branches of saplings or small trees as platforms from which to proclaim their identity, sexual availability (some males are polygamous), and territorial rights.

Palm Warbler *Dendroica palmarum* 5¼ in. **p.200**
Fairly common spring (early April to late May), uncommon fall (mid-Sept. through Oct.) transient.

A ground-loving, tail-bobbing warbler of woodland borders and open, brushy or weedy places. Spring adults have a chestnut cap; yellow eye stripe, throat, and undertail coverts; and yellow to whitish breast, belly, and sides. Breast, sides, and lower side of neck are streaked with chestnut. White spots in corners of tail. Upperparts (except cap) brownish and faintly streaked. Fall birds (see photograph) lack most of the yellow and chestnut, but the undertail coverts remain yellow. Tail-bobbing habit is a good field character both spring and fall (but see Prairie Warbler). Song is a weak, rapid, buzzy trill, all on one pitch.

Bay-breasted Warbler *Dendroica castanea* 5½ in. **p.201**
Uncommon spring (mid-April to late May) and fall (late Aug. through Oct.) transient.

Spring male (see photograph) is striking and unmistakable, with his chestnut head, upper breast and sides, black face and forehead, and large, buff-colored patches on the sides of the neck. The remaining underparts are white to buff, and there are two conspicuous white wing bars. Spring female is duller, lacking the black mask, and with the chestnut much reduced, being noticeable mainly on the sides and flanks. Fall birds have greenish upperparts (except wings and tail), unstreaked underparts, buff undertail coverts, dark legs, and often a chestnut wash on the sides and flanks. Song is a series of high-pitched, hissy notes. Frequents both coniferous and deciduous trees during migration, where it feeds among the lower to topmost branches.

Blackpoll Warbler *Dendroica striata* 5¼ in.
Fairly common spring (mid-April to late May), rare fall (mid-Sept. to mid-Oct.) transient.

The spring male's head is solid black above the level of

119

the eyes. Large, conspicuous white cheeks are bordered below by a black mustache line. Throat, breast, belly, and undertail coverts are white. Bold black streaks occur on the gray back, sides, and sides of neck. Tail and wings are dark gray, with two white wing bars. Spring females resemble the spring males but lack the black cap and white cheeks, and are otherwise generally duller. Fall birds resemble breeding females, but with a distinct greenish-yellow tinge. Light-colored (pink to orange) legs and feet, and white undertail coverts help distinguish fall birds from immature Bay-breasted Warblers. Blackpoll Warbler is a rather sluggish warbler that frequents the middle to upper regions of the trees in which it feeds. Its very high-pitched song is a series of hurried notes, all on one pitch, with the middle notes typically the loudest.

Cerulean Warbler *Dendroica cerulea* 4¹/₂ in.

Fairly common summer (early April through Sept.) resident.

Spring male is blue or blue-gray above and white below, with a narrow black band across the upper breast, blue-black streaks on the sides, and two white wing bars. Females and immatures have a pale yellow breast and throat, a light eyebrow stripe, greenish-gray upperparts, no breast band, and subdued streaking on the sides. Song is a short series of buzzy notes, the last prolonged and usually higher-pitched. Fond of the uppermost levels of the tallest trees, Cerulean Warbler prefers wooded streamsides and the lower slopes of lakeside forests. Its breeding distribution in LBL is spotty, but where they occur they may be common. It is one of the species most guilty of inducing that affliction of birders known as "warbler neck," contracted as one stands for long periods with head tilted fullback, scanning the very tops of the trees overhead, straining for a glimpse of this vocal but elusive bird.

Black-and-white Warbler *Mniotilta varia* 5 in.

Summer resident. Fairly common spring (early April through May) and fall (Aug. to Mid-Oct.); rare summer.

Breeding adults are black, white, and gray. The sides and

top of the head are boldly striped with black and white. The throat is black in males, white in females. There are two white wing bars, and black streaks on the sides and flanks (streaks subdued in females and immatures). Undertail coverts are spotted. The similar spring male Blackpoll Warbler has a solid black cap (instead of a streaked crown), no eyebrow stripe, all white undertail coverts, and lighter-colored legs and feet. The song of Black-and-white Warbler is a series of six or so high-pitched, two-syllabled notes, with the stress on the first syllable of each note: "we'-say, we'-say, we'-say." Black-and-white Warbler is a bark gleaner, and suggests a nuthatch as it deliberately creeps up, down, and around trunks and larger branches in search of insects and spiders. Though LBL is well within the breeding range of this species it apparently is only a rare breeder there.

American Redstart *Setophaga ruticilla* 5 in.
Summer resident. Uncommon spring (mid-April through May) and fall (Sept.), rare summer.

Spring male deep black above except for bright orange patches on wings and outer base of tail. Head, throat, and breast also black. Orange side shows as a patch in front of the bend of the folded wing. Rest of the body underneath is white. Females patterned as males, but with gray or greenish-gray instead of black, yellow instead of orange, white throat and breast, and often a discernible light eyering. Immatures resemble females. Males in first spring also resemble females, but have some black on breast and head, and yellow patches showing some orange. A fidgety bird, it flits about among the foliage of the forest understory, usually near streams or marshes. Fond of spreading tail and wing feathers, thus exhibiting its bright patches (possibly to startle insects into flight). It commonly catches flying insects on the wing, flycatcher-fashion. The song is changeable, but is usually a series of four to six high-pitched, distinct, one-or-two-syllabled notes, with the last note variable in pitch, though usually lower.

Prothonotary Warbler *Protonotaria citrea* 5¹/₂ in. **p.201**
Common summer (early April through Sept.) resident.

In spring the male (see photograph) has a rich, golden-yellow head, neck, breast, belly, and sides. The flanks and hindbelly are more yellow and less golden, and the under-tail coverts are whitish. The back is olive, the rump, wings, and tail bluish-gray. There are no wing bars, but the tail feathers show considerable white when spread. Females and immatures are similar—basically dull versions of the adult male. "Swamp meteor" would be a good name for this noisy, brilliant-yellow bird as it darts among the near-ground vegetation in wooded areas near water. The only warbler in LBL that is a cavity nester; often nests in low, rotten snags, near or over water. Though it may do some cavity excavation work of its own in thoroughly rotten wood (it has a heavy bill for a warbler), it typically uses cavities pre-excavated by other species; crevices and crannies may also be used. Prothonotary Warbler readily adopts nestboxes put up for bluebirds or wrens, some-times at a considerable distance from water. The song is a series of five to eight loud, clear, whistled notes, all on the same pitch, but each note slightly up-slurred: suggests the series of whistles we commonly use to call dogs.

Worm-eating Warbler *Helmitheros vermivorus* 5¹/₄ in.
p.202
Fairly common summer (mid-April through late Sept.) resi-dent.

A drab bird, olive-brown above and buffy beneath, with a conspicuously striped head (black and buff) and pinkish legs and feet. Immatures and females resemble breeding males. Except for its needle-like bill, this species suggests a sparrow in appearance as it forages on and near the ground on wooded, leaf-strewn slopes, often amidst dense undergrowth. The song is insectlike—a buzzy, monotone trill, suggesting the song of Chipping Sparrow, but weaker and faster. It is a ground nester, and has been shown to be especially sensitive to the progressive fragmentation of its deciduous forest home into smaller and smaller parcels. Its name refers to its predilection for worm-like insect lar-vae rather than earthworms.

Swainson's Warbler *Limnothlypis swainsonii* 5¼ in.

Extremely rare spring (mid-April to late May) and fall (late Aug. through Sept.) transient.

Swainson's Warbler looks somewhat like Worm-eating Warbler, but has a solid rusty crown (instead of a striped crown). There is a light eyebrow stripe and a dark eyeline. Adults and immatures are similar. Though LBL is within the known breeding range of Swainson's Warbler, it has not yet been documented as occurring there, and extensive efforts to find it in LBL during the summers of 1988 and 1989 were unsuccessful. Its preferred habitat in the western part of its range—canebrakes and brushy wooded swamps—exists in LBL in several localities. It is included here because of the good possibility that it may be found, since there seems to be appropriate habitat. The song is loud, beginning with three or four clear, whistled notes, these followed by several run-together notes, falling in pitch, and with the last syllable typically on a higher pitch.

Ovenbird *Seiurus aurocapillus* 6 in.

Fairly common summer (mid-April through mid-Oct.) resident.

The upperparts are plain olive, except for the head, which is capped with a dull orange crown bordered on each side by a black stripe. There is a noticeable light eye-ring. The underparts are white, with several rows of bold, black spots on the breast and sides. The white throat is bordered on each side by a dark stripe extending from the base of the bill to the upper breast. Legs and feet are pink, and the birds walk instead of hop (unusual for a warbler). Immatures and adults look alike. Fond of fairly mature deciduous forests with open understory and abundant leaf litter, Ovenbird may be found from moist bottomlands to high up on dry ridge slopes. Because it is elusive, shy, and difficult to get a good look at, we would doubtless believe this bird to be much less common than it is if not for its loud and frequent singing. The song is a series of six to ten loud, emphatic, one- or two-syllabled notes, each note louder than the preceding one (a crescendo, if you please): "pea-cher, pea-cher, pea-cher...," or "peach, peach, peach...." Ovenbird is named for its nest, placed on the forest floor and roofed with twigs and leaves; the opening to the nest cavity is slit-like and on the side of the nest, as in a Dutch oven.

Northern Waterthrush *Seiurus noveboracensis* 5³/₄ in. Uncommon spring (mid-April to late May) and fall (late Aug. through mid-Oct.) transient.

A large, ground-dwelling, walking, teetering warbler, reminiscent of a small sandpiper in its looks, behavior, and choice of habitat. Upperparts brown, with a buff or cream-colored stripe running along each side of the head just above the eye. The underparts are buff, cream, or yellow-ish, with rows of dark brown spots on the breast, sides, and throat (spots on the throat are small). All ages and both sexes are similar. Look for Northern Waterthrush near water, on the ground (often wades in shallow water in a streambed) or in low, sometimes thick, vegetation. The marshy headwater areas of beaver ponds and subimpoundments in LBL are favorite haunts. Tireless singers, with a loud, clear song, beginning on three or so up-slurred notes, progressing quickly into a series of three middle notes, and usually ending in three lower-pitched notes, each of which tends to be slurred downward: "sweet, sweet, sweet, twe, twe twe, choo, choo, choo." Northern Waterthrush is another species that is more easily heard than seen.

Louisiana Waterthrush *Seiurus motacilla* 6 in.   **p.202** Fairly common summer (mid-March to early Oct.) resident.

Similar in appearance to Northern Waterthrush (which does not breed in LBL), Louisiana Waterthrush differs in having a white eye stripe, white throat (though there is a brown "mustache" stripe bordering the throat on each side), and white ground color underneath. Its habits, including teetering, walking instead of hopping, and choice of habitats are also similar, though it is less partial to marshy conditions (preferring instead streamsides) than Northern Waterthrush. Nest is constructed of leaves, in masses of tree roots or beneath bank overhangs, along stream margins. As they search for aquatic insects and other invertebrates in shallow water they often retrieve, flip over, and examine dead leaves and other streambed debris. They have been reported to occasionally catch small minnows. The beautiful song begins with three or four high notes (each slightly upslurred) and then degenerates into a cacophony of jumbled, twittering notes of various pitches, but with an overall tendency to drop in pitch.

Kentucky Warbler *Oporornis formosus* 5$\frac{1}{2}$ n.   p.203
Common summer (mid-April to mid-Sept.) resident.

Upperparts solid olive green, except for black on forehead and crown. There are no wing bars. Underparts solid bright yellow. Black on sides of head and neck, separated from black atop the head by yellow which nearly encircles the eyes and extends forward to base of the bill, gives this species a bespectacled, mustachioed appearance. Sexes are similar, though black of females is less intense. Look for Kentucky Warbler in moist, dense woodlands, especially along waterways and in shaded ravines with moderate to heavy undergrowth. Most of its time is spent on or near the ground, where it feeds and where it builds its nest in a clump of vegetation. It is a favorite host for nest parasitism by Brown-headed Cowbird. The song, resembling some versions of those of Carolina Wren, Ovenbird, and Tufted Titmouse, is a series of rapid, two-syllabled "tur-key, tur-key, tur-key...," or barely three-syllabled "tur-ti-key, tur-ti-key..." notes, each note repeated five to ten times. An incessant singer, it may sing several times a minute throughout most of the day. Though common, it is not easily seen, given its concealing habitat and furtive habits. To appreciate just how common it is you must learn its song.

Connecticut Warbler *Oporornis agilis* 5$\frac{1}{2}$ in.
Rare spring (late April through May) and fall (early Sept. through mid-Oct.) transient.

The spring male has a gray hood that covers the entire head, neck, and upper breast; also has a complete, whitish eye-ring. Upperparts, wings, and tail are solid olive-brown; underparts, except as noted above, are completely yellow. The legs and feet are pink. The breeding female resembles

125

the male but her hood is brown instead of gray. Immatures resemble females, but the eye-ring may not be as white. Connecticut Warbler haunts dense underbrush in wet, forested areas (beaver ponds are good habitat). It is a shy bird. Connecticut Warbler walks, whereas the similar Mourning Warbler hops. The song is loud and clear, a series of several two- or three-syllabled notes, the tempo tending to quicken, and the last note emphasized.

Mourning Warbler *Oporornis philadelphia* 5¹/₄ in.
Rare spring (late April to early June) and fall (late Aug. to late Oct.) transient.

Breeding male resembles Connecticut Warbler male, but lacks the white eye-ring and has a black bib on the upper breast, at the bottom of the gray hood. Adult female resembles adult male but the hood is a lighter shade of gray, the black bib is missing, and a thin, light-colored (but not white) eye-ring may be apparent. Immatures resemble adults of their respective sexes, but are generally paler, with the hood and bib not so well-developed. Mourning Warbler hops (rather than walks) as it forages in the same kinds of habitats preferred by Connecticut Warbler. Both these species are shy, skulking birds, difficult to get a good look at. The song of Mourning Warbler is a series of four to seven loud, liquid, two-syllabled notes, the last few notes on a lower pitch.

Common Yellowthroat *Geothlypis trichas* 5 in. **p.203**
Common summer (early April to early Nov.) resident.

Adult male (see photograph) is olive above and yellow below, except for a whitish belly. A broad, black mask, bordered above and behind by white, extends from one side of the face, across the top of the bill, back to the other side of the face. Females lack the black mask, but have a light eye-ring. Immature males resemble females but may show suggestions of the mask. A lover of marshes, overgrown fields, fencerows, and similar areas of dense vegetation, but never found in woodlands. Its actions, including tail-cocking, are reminiscent of a wren. Though often heard, it is only uncommonly seen because of its habits and habitat. The bulky nest is attached to plant stems, on or near the ground. The song is a loud "witch-a-tee, witch-a-tee, witch-a-tee, witch," or "wit-she, wit-she, wit-she, witch."

Hooded Warbler *Wilsonia citrina* 5¹/₂ in.   **p.204**
Summer resident. Uncommon spring (mid-April to mid-May), rare summer and fall (mid-May to mid-Sept.)

Upperparts olive-green, underparts yellow. No wing bars. Breeding male (see photograph) is aptly named: he has a black hood over head and breast, interrupted by a yellow mask across face and forehead. Females and young lack the hood. Tail white below; white streaks in the outer feathers are visible from above (these white streaks show only when the tail is spread, but the bird has a habit of doing this frequently). Look (or better, listen) for Hooded Warbler in woodlands with dense undergrowth, either near water or well up onto hillsides. It spends most of its time within a dozen feet of the ground, but not much actually on the ground. The nest is typically in a shrub, vine, or small tree, from one to six feet above ground level. The song, loud and distinctive, is a "da-wit, da-wit, da-wit, dee-oh," with the last two-syllabled note emphasized.

Wilson's Warbler *Wilsonia pusilla* 4³/₄ in.
Uncommon spring (late April through May) and fall (mid-Aug. to late Oct.) transient.

A small warbler, solid yellow below and greenish-yellow above. The spring male has a solid black cap. Adult females may have a subdued blackish cap, but the immatures never do. Both females and immatures have a yellowish eyebrow stripe. A very active warbler, rarely seen more than ten feet above the ground. It prefers thickets, often near wet or marshy places. As it seeks insects it sometimes flits its wings. Insects may be captured in mid-air. Song is six to eight chittering notes, dropping in pitch at the end.

Canada Warbler *Wilsonia canadensis* 5¹/₄ in.   **p.204**
Uncommon spring (late April to late May) and fall (Aug. to early Oct.) transient.

The breeding male (see photograph) is solid blue-gray above, including wings and tail, and bright yellow below (except for white undertail coverts). Conspicuous yellow spectacles. There is a bold black "necklace" across the upper breast, and black on the sides of the neck and on the sides of the face beneath the eye. Top of head lightly streaked with black. Females and immatures are similar, but with the necklace and black area of the head much fainter. Look for this warbler in the lower levels of wooded areas where undergrowth is fairly thick, especially near wet or marshy areas. Canada Warbler is fairly active, and sometimes hawks insects on the wing. The song is loud and emphatic, beginning with a low chip, followed by a burst of staccato notes, hardly any two of them on the same pitch.

Yellow-breasted Chat *Icteria virens* 7¹/₄ in.   **p.205**
Common summer (mid-April to mid-Oct.) resident.

This, our largest warbler, is a lover of brushy thickets, briar patches, and heavily overgrown, abandoned fields. Olive-drab above, with bright yellow throat, breast, and sides, and white belly and undertail coverts. The bill is heavy and black. White spectacles, and a short, white stripe extending back from the lower jaw to beneath the eye, accentuate the black (gray in females and immatures) lores and dark cheeks. The tail is longish. Yellow-breasted Chat is a striking bird, both in appearance and vocalizations. Its "song" almost defies description, being a cacophonous but arresting concatenation of whistles, grunts, squeals, squawks, whoops, and caws. Commonly, only single notes are uttered. The sounds, coming from an invisible source deep in a thicket, may suggest that a squabble between more than one species is taking place, but we are fairly certain that this is not the case. Campers are sometimes peeved by the tendency of Yellow-breasted Chat to burst forth with weird single notes, or even full renditions of its song, at all hours of the night—especially when the moon and the androgens are up. The nest is loose and bulky, placed in thick vegetation a few feet above the ground.

128

Summer Tanager *Piranga rubra* 7½ in.   **p.205**
Common summer (mid-April to late Oct.) resident.

The breeding male (see photograph) has bright red plumage over his entire body, except that wings (especially the primaries) and tail show some blackish. The large, "swollen" beak is pale. Female lacks any red, is instead a yellowish-orange everywhere, with wings and tail slightly darker. Male in first spring is a gaudy patchwork of red and greenish-yellow. Look for Summer Tanager in the middle to uppermost layers of deciduous and mixed deciduous-coniferous forests. Singing males often choose conspicuous perches at the very tops of trees. An energetic singer, Summer Tanager's song is a series of short, robin-like phrases, the individual notes slightly less clear (more burry) than in American Robin's song, but less burry than the notes in the very similar song of Scarlet Tanager. The tempo is usually quicker than in American Robin's song. A characteristic and frequently heard call note is "pi-tuck," or "pik-a-tuck," or "pik-a-tuck-a-tuck." In spite of its bright plumage, the male is not easy to see as it forages and sings in the canopy. The tanagers of LBL eat insects, including bees and wasps, which they often catch in mid-air. Some berries and other fruits are also eaten.

Scarlet Tanager *Piranga olivacea* 7 in.   **p.206**
Fairly common summer (mid-April to late Oct.) resident.

The breeding male (see photograph) is indeed scarlet, except for solid black wings and tail. The bill is large and pale. Fall males have the black wings and tail, but are otherwise greenish-yellow. Molting males show a patchwork pattern of scarlet and green. Females and immatures resemble fall males, but wings and tail are brown instead of black. Scarlet Tanager occurs in the same habitats in LBL as does Summer Tanager—the middle to upper layers of deciduous or mixed deciduous-coniferous forests. The songs of these two species are very similar, though the notes of Scarlet Tanager tend to be more burry; a two-syllabled call note—a "chip-urrr," or "chip-baack," the first syllable accented and the second drawn out and lower-pitched—is distinctive of Scarlet Tanager. In the nonbreeding season tanagers feed on berries and other fleshy fruits, in addition to insects.

Northern Cardinal *Cardinalis cardinalis* 8½ in.   **p.206**
Common permanent resident.

One of the most common and most conspicuous song-birds of LBL, Northern Cardinal—or "redbird"—is familiar to almost everyone. Adult males (see photograph) are un-mistakable, with their large, conical bills, black face and throat patch, and otherwise solid red plumage. Even the bill is red. The flaming red crest distinguishes Northern Cardinal from all other predominantly red songbirds of LBL. The female has red restricted to the wings, tail, crest, and bill, though she has the black face and throat patch. Otherwise she is grayish above, buff below. Juveniles look like adult females, but are grayer, have a dark bill, and lack the black face and throat patch. Both sexes sing vari-ous versions of their song, but loud, clear, whistled notes, often with some or all of the notes sliding in pitch, are typi-cal; "witch-ear, witch-ear, witch-ear," or "pretty, pretty, pretty," or "whoit, whoit, whoit," or some combination of these or other phrases, are common. Found throughout LBL except in open grasslands. Feeds on various seeds, fruits, and insects, and is a regular patron of bird feeders. The nest is usually in brushy tangles. Northern Cardinal is a common victim of Brown-headed Cowbird brood para-sitism. In winter, may form foraging flocks of up to several dozen birds.

Rose-breasted Grosbeak *Pheucticus ludovicianus* 7³/₄ in.   **p.207**
Fairly common spring (mid-April to mid-May) and fall (mid-Sept. to mid-Oct.) transient.

Adult male (see photograph) has a large, cream-colored, conical bill, and black head, back, wings, and tail. The rump, undertail coverts, belly, and sides of breast are white. The inner wing has two white wing bars above, and there is a large white patch in the outer wing; the corners of the tail also show some white. The breast sports a trian-gular red patch in its center, and in flight the red wing lin-ings (on the undersurface of the wing) may be seen. Fe-male lacks the black and red of the adult male, is streaked brown above, white to buff below, has brown-streaked breast and sides, and a boldly striped brown and white head. Her wing linings are yellow. The winter male, first fall male, and first spring male all have different plumages, but the large, pale bill and white wing patches are common to all. Rose-breasted Grosbeaks frequent trees near open, brushy areas. With their massive, powerful bills, they are well equipped to crack hard-shelled seeds, but they also eat fruits, insects, buds, and (occasionally) flowers. The beautiful, mellow song reminds me of an accomplished American Robin—a series of short phrases composed of clear, whistled notes, and with a faster tempo than American Robin's song. A distinctive note—a loud, high, slightly raspy "pink" or "ink"—is more commonly heard than the song, and will often betray the presence of an otherwise unnoticed bird.

Blue Grosbeak *Guiraca caerulea* 6³/₄ in.   **p.207**
Fairly common summer (mid-April to early Oct.) resident.

Blue Grosbeak resembles Indigo Bunting, but is noticeably larger, and the male (see photograph) is a duller blue, has two rusty (buff in female) wing bars, and a more massive bill. (See account of Indigo Bunting for basic description.) Blue Grosbeak is commonly found in open to semiopen, brushy places, such as fencerows, roadsides, overgrown fields, thickets, and forest edges. There it feeds on seeds, fruits, and insects. The breeding male is fond of choosing a conspicuous perch, such as a fence, dead snag, or utility wire, and sitting there for several minutes while singing his warble-like song (quite different from Indigo Bunting's song). It reminds me of Purple Finch's song—short phrases, rising and falling in pitch—but is less hurried. When I first started birding in LBL in the mid-1960s I never saw Blue Grosbeaks. Now they are fairly common. Bewick's Wren, on the other hand, was one of the most common wrens of the area then, and now it's rare. No one knows the reasons for these puzzling changes. We've still much to learn about the dynamics of bird populations.

Indigo Bunting *Passerina cyanea* 5¹/₂ in.   **p.208**
Common summer (mid-April through Oct.) resident.

If you see a bird in LBL that is deep blue all over, and slightly smaller than House Sparrow, it has to be a male Indigo Bunting (see photograph). (Blue Grosbeak male has a proportionately larger bill, rusty wing patches, and is slightly larger than House Sparrow. Eastern Bluebird has a thrush-like bill and is blue only on the upperparts.) Female Indigo Buntings are brown above, buffy below, with faint streaking on the breast; they may show traces of blue on wings and tail, and though faint wing bars may be visible, they are not as distinct as in female Blue Grosbeak. Immatures resemble adult females. Molting males are an inelegant patchwork of blue and brown. Indigo Buntings like trees, but not dense forests. Though the nest is placed near the ground in dense weeds and tangles, the males like to have singing perches well above ground. The song is rendered often, all day long, and well into late summer. It is a distinctive series of paired notes, each pair on a different pitch from the preceding. Indigo Bunting is one of several LBL songbirds that seem to benefit from the opening of the forest canopy as a result of timber cutting. Habitat for this species in LBL also increases as abandoned fields revert to woodlands.

Dickcissel *Spiza americana* 6¹/₂ in.
Rare summer (late April to mid-Sept.) resident.

Though LBL is well within the breeding range of Dickcissel, and it is a fairly common summer bird in areas nearby, it is rare in LBL itself. As a bird of extensive, open areas, dominated by grasses, weeds, or scattered brush, it seeks suitable habitat outside LBL (LBL is much more heavily forested than the surrounding region). If present, it is conspicuous because of its loud, distinctive song, sung by males from near-ground perches: "dick, dick, dick-ciss-el." The male Dickcissel is streaked brown above, with a grayish head and sides of breast, a white upper throat, and a black bib on an otherwise yellow breast. The wings have rusty shoulder patches. An eyebrow stripe is yellow in front, becoming white behind the eye. A yellow or white stripe extends back along the lower face from the base of the lower mandible. Sides, belly, flanks, and undertail coverts are dingy white. The female is similar, but has a browner head, less yellow on the face and breast, and lacks the black bib. Dickcissel is a seed eater, but also takes many insects, especially when feeding nestlings. Often nests in loose colonies which tend to move from year to year.

Rufous-sided Towhee *Pipilo erythrophthalmus* 8 in. p.208
Common permanent resident.

A ground-loving bird, often heard scratching in the ground litter in thick brush as it kicks backward with both feet simultaneously, hoping to uncover invertebrates and seeds. It is shy, and never far from brush cover. Adult male (see photograph) with black head, neck, breast, back, wings, and tail. Each wing has a white spot at the base of the primaries; tail corners are also white. The sides and flanks are rufous, the belly white, and the undertail coverts buff. The bill is short, conical, and black; eyes are red. Females similar, but are a rich brown where the male is black. Juveniles have adult wing and tail patterns, but are heavily streaked on head and body with light and dark brown. The full song is a loud, "drink, your, tee-ee-ee-ee-ee," the second note lowest and the third long and quavering. Sometimes the "drink" note is omitted, in which case the translation becomes "tow-heeeee." Common calls include a raspy "che-wink" (second syllable higher). Nests on or near the ground, in dense cover.

American Tree Sparrow *Spizella arborea* 6¹/₄ in.
Rare winter (Nov. through March) resident.

Kin to Chipping and Field Sparrows, adults of this species can be distinguished by their larger size, rusty eyeline (black in Chipping), and dark spot in center of breast. The head is gray, except for a rusty crown, nape, and eyeline. Upperparts are brown, boldly streaked with blackish on the back. There are two white wing bars, and white on the edges of the outer tail feathers. Underparts are light gray (lighter on belly), with buffy sides. American Tree Sparrow lives in brushy or weedy places such as stream margins, fencerows, and abandoned fields. It eats mostly seeds, at least on its winter range. The lovely song begins with one to three high, clear whistles, and then breaks into a sort of warble. For the most part, American Tree Sparrow and Chipping Sparrow do not overlap in their seasonal occurrences in LBL, though Field Sparrow is a permanent resident there.

Chipping Sparrow *Spizella passerina* 5¹/₂ in.   **p.209**
Fairly common summer (mid-March through Oct.) resident.

The rufous crown and nape, white eyebrow stripe, black eyeline, unblemished underparts, dark bill, and small size identify adults of this species (see photograph). The underparts and sides of face are a uniform gray; upperparts as in American Tree Sparrow. Winter birds have a streaked crown, but some rufous may be apparent. The cheek is browner and the bill paler in winter. Chipping Sparrows are unusually tame, especially in residential areas, where they may hop about on the ground within a few feet of passing humans. Much of their food is taken from or near the ground, though singing males often choose perches higher in trees. The nest is a compact cup of rootlets and dried grass, lined with hair, usually in dense shrubs or brushy tangles within a few feet of the ground. Mowed lawns, landscaped with various shrubbery, are favorite summer haunts, and in such places Chipping Sparrow may build its nest within inches of heavy human pedestrian traffic. The song is a mechanical trill, all on one pitch, much like that of Dark-eyed Junco.

Field Sparrow *Spizella pusilla* 5¹/₂ in.   **p.209**
Common permanent resident.

A small sparrow with a rusty cap, pink bill, gray face, white eye-ring, and pink legs and feet. The rusty back is streaked with brown. Underparts are light gray, with a rusty wash on the sides, flanks, and across the breast. The rump is grayish-brown, and the brown wings have two white wing bars. Immatures are similar but duller, have faint streaks on the breast and sides, and buff wing bars. (See accounts of American Tree Sparrow and Chipping Sparrow for tips on distinguishing among these three closely related species.) Field Sparrow prefers open to semiopen areas with brushy thickets or fencerows nearby. It eats seeds, and is a common visitor to bird feeders in the area. The song is lovely—an accelerating series of clear, whistled notes that may rise, fall, or stay on the same pitch toward the end. Song lasts two to three seconds, and is repeated often through much of the day for most of the summer. Summer-long singing is typical of many species that, like Field Sparrow, regularly have two or even three broods in a single season. The well-built cup nest is placed low in grass clumps, brush, or vine tangles.

Vesper Sparrow *Pooecetes gramineus* 6 in.
Uncommon spring (March through April) and fall (late Sept. to mid-Nov.) transient.

Vesper Sparrow, a grayish, heavily streaked bird, prefers the ground and near-ground areas in open or semiopen country. It is predominantly gray or grayish-buff, with brown-streaked back, head, breast, sides, and flanks. The head has a two-toned bill (gray upper mandible, pinkish lower), a white eye-ring, and a brown ear patch bordered below and behind by dingy white. The wings have two faint, buff wing bars, and a rusty shoulder patch (often covered by other feathers when the wing is folded). The blackish tail with its white outer feathers is a good field mark, but unless the bird is flushed the white may be hidden by the overlapping central feathers. When on the ground Vesper Sparrow hops from place to place rather than walks. The song begins with a couple of long, slurred whistles, followed by two higher-pitched notes, these followed by a varied series of short, trilled notes. A useful mnemonic is "here, here, where, where, all-together-down-the-hill." Though the word "vesper" in the common name of this species alludes to its habit of singing at dusk, many other songbirds do as well, and the peak period of singing for Vesper Sparrow is, as in most songbirds, at dawn.

Savannah Sparrow *Passerculus sandwichensis* 5¹/₂ in.
p.210
Uncommon winter (mid-Sept. to mid-May) resident.

A small sparrow of open country, conspicuously streaked with brown on the back, breast, sides, flanks, and head. A yellowish eyebrow stripe is usually evident (though it may be more buff than yellow). There is a light, median crown stripe, and a brown ear patch. Savannah Sparrow lacks the rusty shoulder patch, white outer tail feathers, and eye-ring of Vesper Sparrow; it is also smaller, lacks wing bars, and has pinker legs and feet. Though a central breast spot is occasionally apparent, the shorter, notched tail, characteristic eyebrow stripe, and pinker legs and feet distinguish it from Song Sparrow (which regularly shows a central breast spot). Savannah Sparrow's song begins with two or three short, high, lisping notes followed by two longer, trilled notes, the last one lower-pitched. Though sometimes seen in weedy or brushy surroundings, it is usually not far from open areas dominated by short vegetation or even barren ground, where it forages for seeds. As with several species of small, open-area sparrows, Savannah sometimes scurries, mouselike, along the ground.

Grasshopper Sparrow *Ammodramus savannarum* 5 in.
Rare summer (April through Sept.) resident.

A small, stocky, short-tailed, flat-headed, large-billed sparrow of grasslands and old fields, usually in uplands. Underparts of adult are unstreaked (except, faintly, on the breast), with buff across the breast and on the sides and flanks, and a whitish belly. The back is streaked with dark (brown or chestnut) and light (buff, gray, or white). A light median stripe runs through the dark crown. Wings and lower back may show some rust. The head shows a buff face, a white eye-ring, and often yellow-orange lores. Young birds have a white throat, streaked breast and sides, and show much less buff on the underparts. Grasshopper Sparrow is named for its buzzy, insect-like song, easily overlooked as being the song of a bird. Once learned however, it is distinctive and provides the best clue to the presence of this species. They tend to be semi-colonial in their nesting, and if one singing male is found

136

others are likely to be nearby; in an apparently identical field across the road, they may be absent. The nest is built on the ground beneath concealing vegetation, and though it may survive a hay-cutting operation, it may not survive the risks of increased exposure to predators and weather resulting from the removal of the vegetation cover.

Le Conte's Sparrow *Ammodramus leconteii* 5 in.

Extremely rare spring (mid-March through April) and fall (Oct.) transient.

A small sparrow of grassy or weedy vegetation. The throat, breast, and sides are buff, with streaking restricted to the sides and flanks. The belly is white. A light, median stripe runs through the dark crown. Below the crown is an ocherous-buff eyebrow stripe above a grayish cheek patch. The back is boldly striped with dark brown and buff, and between the crown and back is a distinctive russet-striped, gray nape (only visible at close range). Juveniles resemble adults, but are paler and have streaked breasts. The buzzy song is similar in timbre to that of Grasshopper Sparrow, but is usually broken into two syllables. Though not difficult to approach, Le Conte's Sparrow is difficult to see well because of its habit of staying low in the vegetation and scurrying away on foot or, if forced to fly, going only a short distance before disappearing into the weeds again.

Fox Sparrow *Passerella iliaca* 7 in.   p.210

Uncommon winter (mid-Oct. to mid-April) resident.

A large, reddish sparrow of dense undergrowth and streamside thickets, where it forages in the ground litter by "hop-kicking" like Rufous-sided Towhee. Top of head, nape, and back are gray, streaked with rust. Tail, rump, and wings are rufous. Underparts are heavily spotted with large, rusty, triangular spots, merging into streaks on the sides and flanks, and commonly concentrated as a large spot in the center of the breast. (Hermit Thrush occurs in similar habitats in LBL, and also has a rufous tail, but it has a slimmer, less-conical bill, and lacks the rusty—or "foxy"—look of Fox Sparrow's head and body.) The song is variable, and each male typically has several versions in his repertoire which are rendered in sequence. But all versions are beautiful and melodic, composed of clear, trilled, or slurred whistles (the first note is usually a clear whistle). Feeds on seeds, berries, buds, and invertebrates from the soil surface litter or low vegetation.

Song Sparrow *Melospiza melodia* 6 in.   p.211
Fairly common winter (Oct. through April) resident.

A grayish-brown bird that occurs in a variety of semiopen habitats where brushy or weedy retreats are available. The head has a broad, gray eyebrow stripe, brown crown with a median light stripe, brown line from the eye to the back of the face, and a grayish face patch. The throat is white, bordered by black lines on each side. Dark streaks on the back, wings, and tail are brown, with just a hint of rust (noticeably less rust in wings than Swamp Sparrow). Underparts are white, streaked with brown on the breast, sides, and flanks. The center of the breast typically shows a concentration of dark pigment, though the distinctness of this spot varies among individuals (and juveniles typically lack it). A longish tail with rounded tip is "pumped" up and down as Song Sparrow flies. Three or four clear, whistled notes, followed by a trill or several jumbled notes, characterize most songs of Song Sparrow, but hundreds of versions exist. Its loud "chimp" call note sounds much like the note of House Sparrow. Song Sparrow has nested not far from LBL, and seems to be expanding its breeding range, so it may someday be added to LBL's list of breeding birds.

Lincoln's Sparrow *Melospiza lincolnii* 5³/₄ in.
Rare spring (April through May) and fall (mid-Sept. to mid-Nov.) transient.

The basic account of Song Sparrow's plumage applies also to Lincoln's Sparrow, except as follows: Lincoln's is a tad smaller; is much more finely streaked beneath, and usually lacks a central breast spot; has buff on the lower face, as a band across the breast, and on the sides and flanks; shows a sharp line of demarcation between the streaked breast and the unstreaked belly; often has a narrow, but distinct, buffy eye-ring; and has a thinner black border on the sides of the light throat. Adult Lincoln's is similar to immature Swamp Sparrow, but is buffier and more boldly streaked on breast and sides. Lincoln's Sparrow occurs generally in the same habitats of LBL as does Song Sparrow. Both species commonly pump their tails in short flights, though Lincoln's does it with a little less enthusiasm. Lincoln's Sparrow's song is bubbly, almost warbly, beginning with a few low notes, switching to some higher ones, and finally dropping in pitch on the last few notes.

Swamp Sparrow *Melospiza georgiana* 5½ in.   **p.211**
Common winter (mid-Sept. to mid-May) resident.

Dark and skulky, it is not easy to get a good look at Swamp Sparrow. Breeding adults have a rusty cap, white throat, dingy gray breast, and considerable rufous in their upperparts, wings, and tail. Beneath the reddish cap is a gray eyebrow stripe, over a dark stripe behind the eye, over a brownish-gray ear patch. Faint streaks show on the grayish sides and buffy flanks. The belly is whitish. The back is heavily streaked with black. In winter, adults (see photograph) are buffier underneath, especially on the sides and flanks, and have a gray, median crown stripe. All plumages have the reddish wings and tail, but the solid red cap is present only in breeding adults. Swamp Sparrow is aptly named, and is rarely found far from water, though there must be dense vegetation available for cover. The song is a monotone trill, like Chipping Sparrow's but more liquid, less mechanical, and not as hurried.

White-throated Sparrow *Zonotrichia albicollis* 6-3/4 in.   **p.212**
Common winter (mid-Sept. to late May) resident.

The most common winter sparrow of LBL, the breeding adults are also among the prettiest in both appearance and song. It prefers brushy places, anywhere from lakeside to ridgetop. Upperparts are brown, heavily streaked with black on the back, usually with a rusty wash. The tail and wings are brown, and there are two white wing bars. The dingy gray breast shows little or no streaking. Sides and flanks are gray to olive-buff, sometimes with diffuse streaking. White-throated Sparrow is polymorphic, and adults assume one of two distinct color patterns; the differences involve mainly the head. And the appearance of the head is riveting, especially in the white-striped form (see photograph): the white throat is crisply outlined in gray (or, thinly, in black); the crown is black with a narrow, median white stripe; a light eyebrow stripe is yellow from the base of the bill to the eye (the lores), and white from the eye back; a black line behind the eye separates the white of the eyebrow stripe from the gray of the side of the lower face; the bill is gray. In the tan-striped form (more common in LBL), the head is similar but less striking, having tan in place of white and dark brown in place of black for the head stripes. The two forms freely interbreed. Winter adults resemble breeding birds, but are duller (especially the white-striped form, especially on the head). Immatures have dingy throats, may show faint streaks on the breast, and often lack the yellow lores. The song of White-throated Sparrow is a series of clear whistles, beginning with a long, low note, then a long, higher note, then a series of three lower-pitched, three-syllabled phrases—"oh, sam, pea-bod-y, pea-bod-y, pea-bod-y," or "oh, sweet, Can-a-da, Can-a-da, Can-a-da"—easily mimicked by people who can whistle.

White-crowned Sparrow *Zonotrichia leucophrys* 6³/₄ in.   **p.212**
Rare winter (Oct. to mid-May) resident.
   Though similar to White-throated Sparrow, the adult (see photograph) of this species has a pink bill, broader median stripe through the crown, dingier and less crisply demarcated white throat, and lighter, more immaculate gray on the lower face, sides of neck, nape, breast, and sides. The flanks are grayish buff. Immature birds are similar but have duller grays, and brown-and-tan-striped heads. White-crowned Sparrow seems sleeker than White-throated Sparrow, and tends to perch with its body more erect and its neck more stretched out—especially when on the alert. Anyone trying to learn bird songs soon encounters the problem of geographic variation—or dialects, as they are

known to ornithologists—in the songs of a particular species. Much of what we know about how such dialects are acquired by individual birds is based on studies of this species, which is especially prone to dialect variation. However, most dialects of White-crowned Sparrow begin with one or two rather clear notes, followed by a varied assortment of trills. Brushy woodland borders, thickets, overgrown fields, residential areas, and livestock yards are favored haunts.

Dark-eyed Junco *Junco hyemalis* 6 in.   **p.213**
Common winter (late Sept. through April) resident.

Known as "snowbird" to many local residents, Dark-eyed Junco is a conspicuous member of the winter community of birds in LBL. Adult males are solid slate gray above (in some individuals the back is brownish), including the wings and tail, except for white in the outer tail feathers. The breast, sides, and flanks are also gray, the belly and undertail coverts white. Head and breast are sometimes blackish, giving the bird a hooded appearance; the bill is pinkish. Females and immatures are similar, but much browner in those areas which are gray in adult males. The white outer tail feathers, present in all plumages, are conspicuous in flight, and usually show even in the grounded bird. A ground-loving bird, often seen foraging on open ground, its appearance is distinctive. It regularly visits bird feeders, but prefers to feed on seeds that have been scattered on the ground by other species working the feeder. Dark-eyed Juncos often sing their loose, monotone trill in LBL in late winter or early spring, as hormonal levels are rising and the migrational urge is awakening. When not foraging they commonly choose perches in bushes or the lower branches of trees.

Lapland Longspur *Calcarius lapponicus* 6¼ in.
Extremely rare winter (Nov. through Feb.) resident.

Any sightings of this species in LBL will almost surely be of birds in winter plumage, though a few spring records exist for Kentucky and Tennessee. In whatever plumage, it is a bird of open country, especially plowed fields and short grass meadows, though lakeside mudflats and even beaches may be visited. Look for it mixed in with flocks of Horned Larks in such areas. The winter male (and breeding female) has a buff eyebrow stripe, a crown streaked with buff and black, a grayish-brown ear patch boldly bordered with black, a rufous nape, and usually some black on the throat and sides of neck (precise pattern varies). The underparts are white except for black streaks on the sides and flanks. The back is black-and-buff-streaked, and the blackish wings show some buff on their feather edges. The tail is dark, with extensive white visible in the corners when spread, and is distinctive in all plumages. The conical bill is buff, and often black-tipped (American Pipits and Horned Larks have long, thin, dark bills). Winter females and immatures lack the rufous nape and the black on throat and sides of neck; their breasts are typically buffy and finely streaked. The call note of Lapland Longspur (its song is not likely to be heard in LBL), given either in flight or on the ground, is a distinctive, downslurred whistle—"teeuw," or a harsh, three-syllabled sort of rattle—"tri-di-bit."

Bobolink *Dolichonyx oryzivorus* 7 in.
Uncommon spring (mid-April through May), rare fall (mid-Aug. to mid-Oct.) transient.

The breeding male is unmistakable with his black head, underparts, wings, and tail; large, yellow-buff nape patch; and white rump, upper tail coverts, and shoulder patches. Females, immatures, and males in winter plumage all look rather alike, but very different from the breeding male; they are predominantly buff, have a light bill, and are streaked with brown on the head, back, sides, flanks, and undertail coverts. Though closely related to blackbirds, Bobolink has a more sparrow-like bill (i.e., conical). Female and immature Red-winged Blackbirds look a bit like female, immature, and winter male Bobolinks, but are larger, have heavily streaked breasts and bellies, are predominantly brown rather than buff, and have a slimmer, black bill. Bobolink prefers lush meadows and unmowed hayfields; alfalfa and clover fields are particular favorites. The common name is based on the song, bubbly and enthusiastic, and given often as the male hovers or makes gliding descents above the females. Some of the notes, especially the call note, have a twangy, or banjo-like quality—a sort of "peenk." Bobolink is one of the champion migratory songbirds, spending its winters (make that our winters) in southern South America, and breeding in the northern U.S. and southern Canada.

Red-winged Blackbird *Agelaius phoeniceus* 8½ in.

p.213

Common permanent resident.

Adult males (see photograph) are all black except for red shoulder patches (epaulets) bordered below by yellow. The red may be covered by body feathers when the wing is folded, and is then inconspicuous, though usually some of the yellow border will show. Females and immatures are heavily streaked with tans and browns over most of their heads and bodies. The bill is always dark and sharp-pointed. Immature males, though streaked like females, tend to be darker and usually show some yellow, orange, or red on the shoulder. The song is a three-syllabled "kong-qa-reeeee," with the last syllable higher-pitched and drawn out. In winter, this species may form large, even immense, flocks, usually mixed with other species (Common Grackles, Brown-headed Cowbirds, and European Starlings, primarily) that roost in dense concentrations in groves of trees. During their morning and evening flights to and from their foraging areas, huge flocks may stretch from horizon to horizon. Such concentrations of birds (single flocks may include more than a million individuals) may prove pesky, not only to farmers whose grain is being eaten (though much waste grain is taken), but also to people living near the roosts who would like some peace and quiet at night and would just as soon not have their trees killed by bird wastes. But it should be remembered that, during the nesting season when the birds have dispersed to their breeding grounds and are working dawn-to-dusk catching insects for their ravenous young, people may be beneficiaries as well (though these benefits accrue to many more people than do the damages sometimes caused by the winter flocks).

Eastern Meadowlark *Sturnella magna* 9 in. **p.214**
Common permanent resident.

To an ornithologist, not all black birds are blackbirds, and not all blackbirds are black. Eastern Meadowlark is an example of the latter (European Starling is an example of the former). Eastern Meadowlark is predominantly brown above and yellow below. A bold, black, V-shaped "necklace" extends from the sides of the throat down to the upper breast. The brown upperparts are heavily streaked and spotted with dark brown and buff. Hindbelly, sides, and flanks are buff, streaked with dark brown. The mottled, brown-with-blackish tail has large white patches on its sides, conspicuous in flight. The head is buff to grayish-buff, boldly streaked with dark brown, and has yellow lores. The bill is long and pointed. Open grasslands and meadows are the preferred habitat of Eastern Meadowlark. It feeds mostly on the ground and in low vegetation, but singing birds are fond of higher perches such as low trees, fence posts and wires, and utility lines. The song is a loud, clearly whistled "zee-ooo, zee-ear," the final note lowest in pitch and drawn out. A rattling flight call is given often, as is a characteristic alarm note—a short, buzzy "dzert." The flight is stiff-winged, with alternate flapping and gliding. The domed nest (with side entrance) is placed on the ground, well-hidden in a clump of dense vegetation.

Rusty Blackbird *Euphagus carolinus* 9 in.
Rare winter (late Oct. to early May) resident.

Breeding males of this slender-billed, yellow-eyed blackbird are dull black (little or no iridescence shows) all over. Breeding females are similar, but slate gray instead of black. Immatures and winter adults have a rusty crown, back, and breast, gray to black tail and wings (the edges of the wing feathers are often rusty), a conspicuous buff eyebrow line, black lores, and a dark line extending back from the eye. There is a rusty ear patch, and the throat is buff to gray to blackish. The tail is of medium length. The only other yellow-eyed blackbird of LBL is Common Grackle, which is distinctly larger and has a proportionately longer tail (juvenile Rustys have a brown eye, but it is yellow by November). Wooded swamps are the preferred habitat of

Rusty Blackbirds, though they also occur along wooded streamsides and lake margins. Their diet reflects this fondness for water, in which they may sometimes wade as they search for snails, crustaceans, tadpoles, salamanders, and even fish. They also eat various seeds, and sometimes scour cultivated fields for waste grain. Winter blackbird roosts in the LBL region usually contain a few Rustys, but recognizing them in the tumult of such a flock is not easy. The song is a harsh "creak" that has been likened to the sound of a rusty gate hinge (though I believe the name refers instead to the winter color).

Common Grackle *Quiscalus quiscula* 12½ in. **p.214**
Common permanent resident.

This is the largest blackbird in LBL (but not the largest black bird). It also has the longest tail of any LBL blackbird, proportionately as well as absolutely. Adults at a distance appear solid black, but at close range and in good light the males (see photograph) can be seen to be highly iridescent—violet purple on the head, neck, and upper breast, and bronzy on the rest of the body. The tail is widest near its tip rather than at its base, producing a rather "club-tailed" appearance, especially in males. The tail is also unusual in that its feathers form a shallow "V," like the keel of a boat, in cross section; in displaying males it may be a fairly deep "V." Young birds of both sexes are a dull, sooty brown, and have dark eyes until mid-fall. Common Grackles are gregarious, and it is unusual to encounter single birds. Their social nature carries over into their nesting habits as well, and loose nesting colonies, often in coniferous trees, are typical. In winter they are one of four common species that make up the huge winter roosts of the region (see account of Red-winged Blackbird for more information on these "blackbird" roosts). Wooded to semiopen areas are the usual habitat of Common Grackle, but in the nonbreeding season they are not as particular about habitat if there is food to be had. They are indiscriminate feeders, and their list of dietary items is long; bird's eggs and nestlings are on that list, and they commonly scavenge at garbage dumps and picnic grounds, and will even pirate food from other birds. The song (I suppose you could call it that) is a raspy, wheezy, up-slurred "ssh-ga-leek." They also have a loud "chack" note.

Brown-headed Cowbird *Molothrus ater* 5¹/₂ in.   **p.215**
Common permanent resident.

The smallest blackbird of LBL, adult males (bird at top in photograph) are glossy black everywhere, except for a brown head. Females (bird at bottom in photograph) are all gray, and may be faintly streaked below. Juveniles resemble females, but are more distinctly streaked. Males molting into their first adult plumage are a patchwork of black, gray, and buff. Brown-headed Cowbird has prospered since the arrival of Europeans on this continent. The clearing of the forests and introduction of domestic livestock have divorced this species from its original association with bison and allowed it to extend its range into vast areas where it did not previously occur. Its habit of brood parasitism (never building a nest of its own, but laying its eggs in the nests of other species to be incubated and reared by the foster parents) has given it a bad reputation among many bird lovers. But it is a native species in North America, at least in a substantial part of its present range, and many host species seem able to absorb the costs to their reproductive success caused by Brown-headed Cowbird's "nasty" habit. More than 200 host species, from hummingbirds to woodpeckers, gulls, ducks, and even hawks have been reported, though only about two-thirds of the total are known to have ever successfully fledged young cowbirds from their nests. Other songbirds, however, are the most frequent hosts, and several of them, especially in areas where Brown-headed Cowbird did not formerly occur, have been seriously or even disastrously affected. But cowbird eggs face bleak prospects too; their chances of producing nestlings that survive to fledging have been estimated to be less than 1 in 30. The song, often given from exposed perches at the tops of trees, is a high-pitched, gurgling, three-note affair, the last note highest and drawn out: "glug, glug, gleeeee."

Orchard Oriole *Icterus spurius* 6-3/4 in.   **p.215**
Common summer (early April through Sept.) resident.

The common summer oriole of LBL, Orchard Oriole prefers wooded areas, but avoids dense forests. Orchards, treed lawns, and woodland edges are good places to seek it, and it is one of several species in LBL that take advantage of the opening of the forest canopy caused by selective cutting of trees. The head, throat, upper back, wings, and tail are black in the adult male (see photograph). The remaining underparts, lower back, rump, and upper tail coverts are deep chestnut. The wing linings are also chestnut, and each wing has a chestnut shoulder patch. Females are mostly greenish-yellow, but darker above, with grayish back, wings, and tail, and two whitish wing bars on each wing. First year males look like females except for a black "bib" on the throat and center of the upper breast (often also on the face), and occasionally some chestnut on the breast. The loud, energetic, and jumbled song—a mix of harsh notes and clear whistles—reminds me of a robust Purple Finch's song; a harsh, downslurred "wheer" note toward the end of the song is distinctive. Orchard Orioles construct a woven nest of grasses suspended between a small fork of a limb well out from the main trunk, but the nest is more of an open cup and less pendulous than that of Northern Oriole. The diet is mostly insects and small fruits.

Northern Oriole *Icterus galbula* 8 in.   **p.216**
Summer resident. Uncommon spring (mid-April through May) and fall (mid-Aug. to mid-Oct.), rare summer.

This species is noticeably larger than Orchard Oriole. The adult male (see photograph) has a black head, throat, back and upper breast. Wings and tail are also mostly black (though each wing has a yellow-orange shoulder patch, yellow linings, and a broad white wing bar, and the tail has large yellow corner patches and yellow undersurface). Otherwise the adult male is bright orange to yellowish-orange. Adult female is grayish-olive above, with gray wings bearing two white wing bars. Her underparts are yellowish-orange, usually with a more distinctly orange cast to the breast and undertail coverts. The first year male resembles adult males, but the orange is duller and the black tends to be splotchy. Though a rare nester in LBL, Northern Oriole builds one of the most impressive nests of any bird in the area. It is a deep, tightly woven, pendulous structure, placed well out on some small, drooping branch, fairly secure from all but the most agile climbing predators. The subspecies (or race) of Northern Oriole that occurs in LBL is still properly known as Baltimore Oriole, though that name is no longer used by ornithologists to denote the entire species. The reason for the change in name is that we now know that Baltimore Oriole and Bullock's Oriole (a western race, formerly considered to be a separate species) interbreed freely in areas where they both occur; that fact, by definition, means that the two forms are members of a single species (the situation is not quite that simple, but almost). Northern Oriole's song is a series of loud, clear whistles and warbled notes, with much variation in the overall arrangement.

Purple Finch *Carpodacus purpureus* 5³/₄ in.   **p.216**
Fairly common winter (Oct. through April) resident.

Purple was an unfortunate choice of adjective for this bird's name—raspberry would have been better, or burgundy. The adult male (bird at top in photograph) is a raspberry-red over much of his body, especially his head, breast, and rump. The wings and tail are brownish, and the back is brown-streaked, but all have a distinct rosy suffusion. Belly and undertail coverts are white, and the flanks are lightly streaked with brown. First year males, immature birds, and adult females (bird at bottom in photograph) are brownish above, whitish below, heavily streaked with brown. The head has a light eyebrow stripe, a dark ear patch, and a dark mustache line. (See account of House Finch for tips on how to distinguish these two closely related species.) Purple Finch loves treetops, where small flocks may be seen moving about rather sluggishly in search of various seeds (their dietary staple, though insects, fruits, and buds are also eaten). They are common diners at bird feeders. House Finch, which just arrived in the region in the 1980s, is reported to be more aggressive and, in spite of its slightly smaller size, may displace Purple Finch from feeders. The song of Purple Finch is an energetic warble, scurrying up and down the scale; individual notes are often slurred, and likely to be repeated once or twice.

House Finch *Carpodacus mexicanus* 5¹/₂ in.
Rare winter (Oct. through April) resident.

Just a bit smaller than Purple Finch, this western species was introduced into the northeastern U.S. in the 1940s and has been expanding its range westward ever since. It was first recorded from Tennessee in 1972, and from Kentucky in 1977. Common in winter in many parts of Kentucky and Tennessee, it is also now breeding in many parts of those two states and apparently will soon be a regular breeder throughout both of them. Very similar to Purple Finch (see account of that species for basic description), but the red of the adult male House Finch is brighter, and the cap, nape, back, wings, and tail are black. The flanks and belly are streaked with brown. The red (or orange, or yellow—individuals vary) is more discretely localized than in Purple Finch, being more or less restricted to the forehead, eyebrow stripe, lower face, throat, breast, and rump. Comparing adult males of the two species, it's almost as if Purple Finch had been spray-painted from above and in front of its head, with an extra squirt added to the rump, and House Finch was a paint-by-numbers product. Females and immatures have a smaller bill than their Purple Finch counterparts, and a more evenly brown head (they lack the ear patch and mustache line). As a lover of urban and suburban areas, House Finch will likely not find most of LBL to its liking, but feeding stations may well attract it, especially in winter. The song is similar to that of Purple Finch, but is less hurried, ranges the scale more, and is, on average, higher-pitched.

Red Crossbill *Loxia curvirostra* 6 in.
Extremely rare winter (Nov. through March) resident.

Red Crossbill has a cone-opener attached to the front of its face, which is convenient for a bird specializing in opening the cones of various evergreen trees in order to feed

149

on the contained seeds. The crossed mandibles are unique among LBL's birds (though it is conceivable that White-winged Crossbill may someday be found there), but you must be fairly close to the bird to actually see that they are crossed. The plumage of the adult male is typically dull red, except for blackish wings and tail. The particular shade of red varies from male to male, and some are even yellow. Typical females are olive yellow or grayish-olive, with dark wings and tail, and a gray throat (all adult males have either yellow or reddish throats). Juveniles resemble females but are duller and distinctly streaked. A typical "erratic finch" in its winter distribution, it is surely not a regular member of LBL's winter bird community. But in "irruption" years, it may well find LBL, with its many pine stands and sweet gum trees, to be a suitable feeding ground. When working pine cones or sweet gum balls for seeds, Red Crossbills tend to be silent, and betray their presence only visually or by the popping noises made by the opening of the cones. They work the cones intently, and get into whatever position they need to (commonly upside down) as they clamber, parrot-like, over and around the cones to get into position to use their specialized bills. In flight, they utter a short series of "chip" or "kip" notes. The song is varied, but usually contains whistles, trills, and warbles.

Pine Siskin *Carduelis pinus* 5 in.   p.217
Uncommon winter (Oct. to mid-May) resident.

Though small and plain, Pine Siskin is nonetheless likely to be noticed when present because it is noisy, quite animated, and usually in flocks. During some winters it is absent from LBL, but in others it may be fairly common. Both sexes are conspicuously streaked on the head, back, breast, sides, flanks, and parts of the belly (brown on tan above, brown on white below). Wings and tail are dark, the latter distinctly notched and with a small yellow patch on each side near its base. The wings have a yellow stripe that runs through the bases of the flight feathers; when folded some of this yellow may show as a small yellow wing patch. The bill is unusually long and thin for a finch, and sharply pointed. Pine Siskins forage in flocks, often moving from site to site in unison, as though the entire flock were being buffeted by some strong, imperceptible wind. They feed on various small seeds, from conifers to grasses, and are regular visitors to bird feeders in irruption years. A long, high-pitched, upward-slurred note is distinctive, and one of the easiest ways to detect the bird's presence in an area—a sort of "zhreeee," or "zeeeet." The song is very much like American Goldfinch's, but wheezy, and often includes the characteristic "zhreeee" note. Pine Siskin is quite tame, and one of the easiest birds to train to take seeds from your hand at a feeding station.

American Goldfinch *Carduelis tristis* 5 in.　　　**p.217**
Common permanent resident.

Males of this species, known as "wild canary" to many local residents, are unmistakable in breeding plumage (see photograph). Their bodies are all bright yellow, except for white under and upper tail coverts. The head too is yellow, with a black cap. The conical bill is flesh-colored, as are the legs and feet (this conical bill shape is not shared by any of the small, yellowish warblers). Wings are mostly black, but there are two white wing bars, white edges on the secondaries, and a yellow-to-olive shoulder patch. The tail is black, with a white margin. Many familiar with the male in summer dress do not recognize it as the same species when it appears at their winter feeders in its comparatively drab winter plumage. Breeding females are yellowish below, olive above, and lack the black cap of breeding males. Wings and tail of females are as in males. Winter birds resemble breeding females, but are grayer. American Goldfinch feeds on small seeds and insects, seeking them at any level from the treetops to the ground. Winter flocks may number in the hundreds, and they commonly mix with Pine Siskin in years when that species appears in LBL. The young are fed mostly a regurgitated pulp of seeds, and nesting is usually not begun before July, thus assuring a good supply of seeds for feeding the nestlings. The tightly woven, cup-shaped nest is placed in a branch fork and lined with thistle down, which is not readily available in LBL before July. The flight of American Goldfinch is very undulating, or roller-coasterish, and in flight the birds often give their characteristic "per-chick-o-ree" call. The song is a jumbled affair, rather high-pitched, of twitters, whistles, and trills, often containing a "sweeee" note.

Evening Grosbeak *Coccothraustes vespertinus* 8 in.
Rare winter (Oct. to early May) resident.

Evening Grosbeak has a massive bill and a quite chunky body. Adult males are dark brown on the head (the crown may be nearly black) with a yellow forehead connecting two yellow eyebrow stripes. The huge bill is cream-colored, sometimes with a greenish tinge. The brown of the head continues onto the body, but gradually changes to bright yellow on the belly, flanks, lower back, and rump. The tail is solid black, stubby, and notched. The black wings show a quadrangular white patch on the secondaries. Females are mostly grayish, with yellow present only as a smidgin here and there on the body (especially the nape and sides of breast). Females also differ from adult males in having white in the tail and an additional white wing patch on the inner primary bases. A classic "erratic finch," Evening Grosbeak may not be seen in an area for several winters, and then show one winter in considerable numbers. It feeds in winter on plant buds and larger seeds, and is especially fond of sunflower seeds at feeders. Its call note—a loud, almost-two-syllabled "cle-erp" or "che-erp"—is distinctive, and suggests House Sparrow's call. Song is a sort of wandering warble.

House Sparrow *Passer domesticus* 6 in.
Common permanent resident.

This familiar species, which probably evolved in the vicinity of the Mediterranean Sea, was brought to this country between about 1850 and 1870 in several deliberate attempts to establish it as a breeding species. Though some of the earliest introductions failed, eventually things started to click and the rest, as the saying goes, is history. From its own perspective it represents one of the notable success stories (in terms of growth of its numbers and expansion of its range) of any bird species anywhere in the world over the last 150 years or so. Breeding males are brown above, the back streaked with black, and are light gray below. The head sports a gray cap and ear patch, a broad, chestnut stripe behind the eye, black lores, whitish cheeks, black throat, and thick, black bill. A black bib on the upper breast connects with the black throat. City folks are sometimes surprised at how handsome breeding males of this species are when unsullied by urban grime. Winter males have a much reduced black bib, and lighter-colored bills. Each wing has a single white wing bar. Females and immatures are brown above, with streaked backs, dingy gray underparts, a pale eyebrow stripe behind the eye, and light bills. House Sparrow is a "weed" among birds, and its aggressive, pugnacious nature has made it the bane of several native species. It competes, usually successfully, with native cavity-nesting species such as bluebirds, wrens, chickadees, and titmice for nest sites. Unlike its weedy compatriot European Starling, it sticks pretty much to areas around sites of human activity. It is therefore an uncommon bird in much of LBL. Though quite vocal, it has nothing that most of us would care to call a song. It chatters, twitters, and chirps.

COLOR PLATES

The color photographs which follow are of adult birds in breeding plumage, except as noted in the captions. Pictures made at the nest of species which do not breed, or are not known to breed, in Land Between The Lakes are also noted in the captions. Since the scale varies among the photographs, the reader should refer to the sizes given in the species accounts when making size comparisons of birds in different photographs.

Pied-billed Grebe — Winter plumage. p. 18

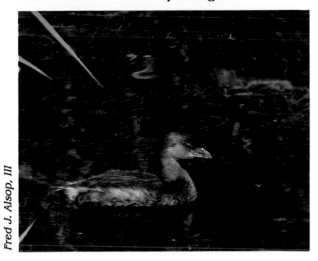

Fred J. Alsop, III

Great Blue Heron p. 22

G. Ron Austing

Great Egret

Fred J. Alsop, III

Little Blue Heron

Fred J. Alsop, III

Green-backed Heron

p. 25

Fred J. Alsop, III

Canada Goose

p. 27

David H. Snyder

157

Wood Duck — Male. **p. 28**

Mallard — Male. **p. 30**

Northern Pintail — Male left, female right. **p. 30**

David H. Snyder

Redhead — Female left, male right. **p. 34**

Fred J. Alsop, III

Ring-necked Duck — Male. **p. 35**

G. Ron Austing

Lesser Scaup — Male. **p. 36**

G. Ron Austing

Common Goldeneye — Male.   **p. 37**

G. Ron Austing

Bufflehead — Male.   **p. 37**

G. Ron Austing

Hooded Merganser — Male, displaying crest. **p. 38**

G. Ron Austing

Common Merganser — Male. **p. 38**

G. Ron Austing

Turkey Vulture p. 41

G. Ron Austing

Osprey — Female. p. 42

G. Ron Austing

Bald Eagle

p. 43

Fred J. Alsop, III

Northern Harrier — Female left, male right (in midmolt from immature to adult plumage).

p. 43

Fred J. Alsop, III

Sharp-shinned Hawk

p. 44

Fred J. Alsop, III

Red-shouldered Hawk

p. 45

Fred J. Alsop, III

Fred J. Alsop, III

Fred J. Alsop, III

American Kestrel — Male.　　　　　　　　　　p. 48

Fred J. Alsop, III

Wild Turkey — Male, gobbling.　　　　　　　p. 49

G. Ron Austing

Northern Bobwhite — Female bottom, male top.   **p. 50**

American Coot   **p. 52**

Fred J. Alsop, III

G. Ron Austing

G. Ron Austing

Spotted Sandpiper — No nesting records for LBL. **p. 57**

G. Ron Austing

Least Sandpiper

p. 59

G. Ron Austing

Pectoral Sandpiper

p. 61

G. Ron Austing

Common Snipe
p. 63

G. Ron Austing

American Woodcock
p. 63

Fred J. Alsop, III

Ring-billed Gull   p. 65

G. Ron Austing

Mourning Dove   p. 68

Fred J. Alsop, III

Yellow-billed Cuckoo
p. 69

G. Ron Austing

Eastern Screech-Owl
p. 70

Fred J. Alsop III

Great Horned Owl

p. 71

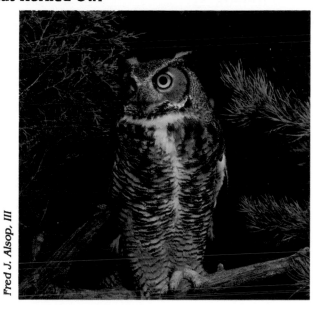

Fred J. Alsop, III

Barred Owl

p. 71

Fred J. Alsop, III

Common Nighthawk — Male.

p. 72

G. Ron Austing

Whip-poor-will

p. 73

G. Ron Austing

Fred J. Alsop, III

Fred J. Alsop, III

G. Ron Austing

Red-headed Woodpecker p. 76

Fred J. Alsop, III

Red-bellied Woodpecker — Female.   **p. 77**

Fred J. Alsop, III

Downy Woodpecker — Male.   **p. 78**

G. Ron Austing

Hairy Woodpecker — Male.   p. 79

G. Ron Austing

Northern Flicker — Female.   p. 79

Fred J. Alsop, III

Pileated Woodpecker — Adult is male.   **p. 80**

Fred J. Alsop, III

Eastern Wood-Pewee   **p. 81**

G. Ron Austing

Acadian Flycatcher

G. Ron Austing

Least Flycatcher — Does not nest in LBL.

Fred J. Alsop, III

Eastern Phoebe

p. 83

Fred J. Alsop, III

Great Crested Flycatcher

p. 84

G. Ron Austing

Eastern Kingbird

p. 84

Fred J. Alsop, III

Horned Lark

p. 85

Fred J. Alsop, III

Purple Martin — Female. p. 86

Fred J. Alsop, III

Tree Swallow — Male. p. 86

G. Ron Austing

Cliff Swallow   **p. 87**

David H. Snyder

Barn Swallow   **p. 88**

Fred J. Alsop, III

Blue Jay p. 89

Fred J. Alsop, III

American Crow p. 89

G. Ron Austing

Carolina Chickadee — On right. **p. 90**
Tufted Titmouse — On left. **p. 91**

Fred J. Alsop, III

White-breasted Nuthatch **p. 92**

Fred J. Alsop, III

Brown Creeper — Does not nest in LBL.   **p. 92**

Fred J. Alsop, III

Carolina Wren   **p. 93**

Fred J. Alsop, III

Blue-gray Gnatcatcher — Male. p. 97

G. Ron Austing

Eastern Bluebird — Male. p. 98

Fred J. Alsop, III

Swainson's Thrush

p. 99

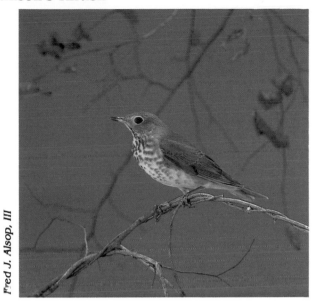

Fred J. Alsop, III

Wood Thrush

p. 101

Fred J. Alsop, III

American Robin — Male.
p. 101

Fred J. Alsop, III

Gray Catbird
p. 102

G. Ron Austing

Northern Mockingbird

p. 102

Fred J. Alsop, III

Brown Thrasher

p. 103

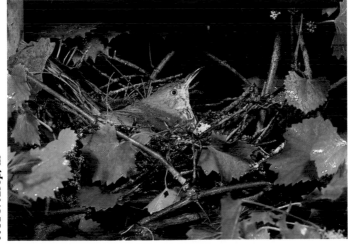

Fred J. Alsop, III

Cedar Waxwing

p. 104

Fred J. Alsop, III

Loggerhead Shrike

p. 105

Fred J. Alsop, III

European Starling
p. 106

Fred J. Alsop, III

White-eyed Vireo
p. 106

Fred J. Alsop, III

Fred J. Alsop, III

G. Ron Austing

Golden-winged Warbler —

p. 110

Male. Does not nest in LBL.

Fred J. Alsop, III

Northern Parula — Female.

p. 112

Fred J. Alsop, III

Yellow Warbler — Male. p. 112

Fred J. Alsop, III

Chestnut-sided Warbler — p. 113
Female. Does not nest in LBL.

Fred J. Alsop, III

Yellow-rumped Warbler — Winter adult.   **p. 115**

Fred J. Alsop, III

Black-throated Green Warbler —   **p. 116**
Male. Does not nest in LBL.

Fred J. Alsop, III

Fred J. Alsop, III

Fred J. Alsop, III

Bay-breasted Warbler —
Male. Does not nest in LBL.

p. 119

Fred J. Alsop, III

Prothonotary Warbler — Fall plumage.

p. 121

Fred J. Alsop, III

Worm-eating Warbler

p. 122

Fred J. Alsop, III

Louisiana Waterthrush

p. 124

Fred J. Alsop, III

Fred J. Alsop, III

Common Yellowthroat — Male.   p. 126

Fred J. Alsop, III

Hooded Warbler — Male. **p. 127**

Fred J. Alsop, III

Canada Warbler — Male. Does not nest in LBL. **p. 128**

Fred J. Alsop, III

Fred J. Alsop, III

Summer Tanager — Male.   p. 129

G. Ron Austing

Scarlet Tanager — Male. p. 129

G. Ron Austing

Northern Cardinal — Male. p. 130

Fred J. Alsop, III

Rose-breasted Grosbeak —
Male. Does not nest in LBL.

p. 130

Fred J. Alsop, III

Blue Grosbeak — Male.

p. 131

Fred J. Alsop, III

Indigo Bunting — Male.
p. 132

Fred J. Alsop, III

Rufous-sided Towhee — Male.
p. 133

Fred J. Alsop, III

Fred J. Alsop, III

Fred J. Alsop, III

Savannah Sparrow — Does not nest in LBL.

p. 136

Fred J. Alsop, III

Fox Sparrow

p. 137

Fred J. Alsop, III

Song Sparrow — Not known to nest in LBL.

p. 138

G. Ron Austing

Swamp Sparrow

p. 139

G. Ron Austing

Fred J. Alsop, III

Fred J. Alsop, III

Dark-eyed Junco

p. 141

Fred J. Alsop, III

Red-winged Blackbird — Male.

p. 143

G. Ron Austing

Eastern Meadowlark

p. 144

Fred J. Alsop, III

Common Grackle — Male.

p. 145

G. Ron Austing

Brown-headed Cowbird —
Female bottom, male top.

Fred J. Alsop, III

Orchard Oriole — Male.

Fred J. Alsop, III

Northern Oriole — Male.   **p. 147**

Purple Finch — Female bottom, male top.   **p. 148**

Fred J. Alsop, III

American Goldfinch — Male. **p. 151**

G. Ron Austing

GLOSSARY

Accipiter–Any of a group of forest-loving hawks which have long, parallel-sided tails and short, rounded wings. Extremely agile, they can fly through surprisingly dense vegetation in pursuit of small birds (their dietary staple). Sharp-shinned Hawk and Cooper's Hawk are the accipiters included in this book. Also called "bird hawks" and "true hawks."

Androgen–The male sex hormone.

Bar–A contrasting mark on the plumage with its long axis perpendicular to the long axis of the body (or wing, in the case of wing bars).

Belly–That portion of the underparts of a bird located below the flanks and sides, before the undertail coverts, and behind the breast.

Bend of the wing–See **wrist**.

Breast–That portion of the underparts of a bird located below the sides, before the belly, and below the neck.

Buteo–Any of a group of hawks with stout bodies, broad wings, and fan-shaped tails. Not as agile as accipiters, they are fond of soaring in the open skies, sometimes so high that they appear as mere specks to the naked eye. Buteos treated in the species accounts are Red-shouldered Hawk, Broad-winged Hawk, Red-tailed Hawk, and Rough-legged Hawk. Also called "buzzard hawks."

Canopy–The uppermost layer of vegetation in a forest.

Crest–An extension of feathers from the back of the crown.

Crown–The top of the head.

Dabbling duck–Any of several species of ducks that rarely dive beneath the water's surface (though most can), that can take flight by springing directly into the air from the water (or land), and that commonly feed by submerging their heads as their rear ends point skyward (called "tipping up," "upending," or "dabbling"). Most dabblers have a brilliantly colored, often iridescent, quadrangular patch (speculum) on the upper surface of the secondary wing feathers, present in both sexes. In this book the dabbling ducks are Wood Duck through American Wigeon in the species accounts. Also called "marsh ducks" and "puddle ducks."

Diving duck–Any of several species of ducks that regularly dive beneath the water's surface to feed or to escape enemies. Their legs are placed relatively far back on their bodies. In taking off from the water they must "taxi" along its surface for some distance. In this book the diving ducks are Canvasback through Bufflehead in the species accounts.

Dorsal–At or toward the top.

Ear tufts–Elongated feathers which extend conspicuously above the other head feathers, and located above, and sometimes to the sides of, the eyes. Among the birds treated in this book, ear tufts are most conspicuous in Eastern Screech-Owl and Great Horned Owl, but small ear tufts also occur in Horned Larks. Also called horns, they are inapparent when laid back against the surrounding feathers.

Empid–Birder's term for any flycatcher of the genus *Empidonax*. All are small, with two light wing bars and a light eye-ring. Difficult to distinguish, but each has a distinctive song, and they prefer different habitats. In this book the empids include Acadian Flycatcher through Least Flycatcher in the species accounts.

Eyebrow–A stripe aside the bird's head at the level of the upper margin of the eye.

Eyeline–A horizontal line on the head of a bird at the level of the eye.

Eye-ring–A circle of contrastingly colored feathers surrounding the eye; it may be either complete or incomplete (interrupted).

Facial disc–A distinct region on the faces of owls, typically flattened, rounded on its margins, and often with a border of some contrasting color. Facial discs are believed to be useful in locating sound sources, such as those produced by a mouse scurrying through dry leaves.

Falcon–Any of a group of hawks with moderately long, relatively narrow, sharply pointed wings ("high speed" wings), and longish tails. Falcons are swift and agile fliers. Only American Kestrel is treated in this book, but Merlin and Peregrine Falcon may rarely visit LBL.

Field character–See **field mark**.

Field mark–Some feature of a bird that is especially useful in identifying its species under field conditions. Same as field character.

Flank–That portion of a bird's underparts located behind the side, above the abdomen, and below the rump.

Flight feathers–The large, main feathers of the wings and tail. Those attached to the outer section of the wing (that section beyond the wrist) are termed primaries. Primaries are attached to that section of the wing supported by metacarpals and phalanges. Secondaries are flight feathers of the inner section of the wing, between the primaries and the body; they are supported by a bone called the ulna.

Forewing–The front, or leading, portion of the wing.

Goatsucker–Any member of the group (order) of birds which includes the nighthawks, nightjars, frogmouths, and their relatives. In this book the goatsuckers are Common Nighthawk, Whip-poor-will, and Chuck-will's-widow.

"Hawk" insects–As a verb, to hawk insects means to sit on a lookout perch, fly out and catch passing insects in mid-air, and then (typically) to return to the same or some nearby perch to consume the insect. Flycatchers are especially good at it, but several other kinds of birds also regularly do it.

Hindbelly–The posterior portion of the belly.

Horns–See **ear tufts**.

Immaculate–Of a solid color with no markings.

Immature–A bird which has not attained its fully adult plumage.

Insectivorous–Insect eating.

Invertebrate–An animal without a backbone.

Irruption–An irregular increase in numbers of a species in an area.

Lateral–At or toward the side.

Lore–The area of a bird's head between the base of the bill and the eye.

Mandible–The bill or beak of a bird. The upper mandible is the upper bill, the lower mandible is the lower bill.

Mantle–An area of the upper surface of birds which includes the back, the feathers above the shoulder (the scapulars), and the upper surface of the wing exclusive of the flight feathers. Used especially with reference to gulls.

Margin–The edge or near-edge of something.

Median–At or toward the middle.

Metacarpals–Bones supporting the inner part of the outer wing, corresponding to the bones of the palm of our hand.

Nape–The back of the neck.

Nectary–A nectar reservoir of a flower.

Omnivorous–Eating both plant and animal matter.

Peep–Birder's term for any sparrow-sized sandpiper.

Phalanges–Bones supporting the outer part of the outer wing, corresponding to our finger bones.

Posterior–At or toward the back end.

Primaries–See **flight feathers**.

Race–See **subspecies**.

Radius–One of two bones supporting the inner wing, corresponding to our own radius (the long bone on the thumb side of our forearm).

Raptor–A bird of prey. The term is usually restricted in usage to denote members of the order of birds which includes the accipiters, eagles, kites, Osprey, falcons, buteos, harriers, and caracaras (the "diurnal raptors"), and the order which includes the owls (the "nocturnal raptors"). Not included are several birds with raptorial habits, e.g., the shrikes and jaegers, which are not technically members of either of those two orders. From a

Latin root meaning "to seize by force; plunder" (the same root serves for "rape" and "rapacious").

Rump–The posterior region of a bird's upperparts, located behind the back, before the uppertail coverts, and above the flanks.

Scavenger–An animal that feeds on dead, often decaying, matter.

Secondaries–See **flight feathers**.

Species–A group of birds which are capable of interbreeding with one another. (The concept of species is actually much more complicated and interesting than that. Applying the concept to real-life situations is sometimes difficult, in substantial part at least because of the ongoing evolutionary process which may change the nature, and therefore the identity, of species through time, or cause a split of one species into two or more.)

Speculum–A brilliantly colored, often iridescent, rectangular patch on the upper surface of the secondaries, especially in dabbling ducks.

Stripe–A contrasting mark on the plumage with its long axis parallel to the long axis of the body (or wing, in the case of wing stripes).

Subspecies–A genetically distinct subset of a species, which is geographically segregated (during the breeding season at least) from other subspecies of the same species. Different subspecies of a single species usually differ in appearance, often enough to permit discrimination among them in the field. But they are not reproductively isolated from one another in areas where their breeding ranges abut, and interbreeding of subspecies in those areas is normal. Also called "race."

Subterminal–Just before the tip.

Summer visitant–A residency status category that includes species which appear in an area in summer, but after the breeding season, and which leave the area before winter.

Teetering–A behavioral trait in which a standing bird repeatedly and rapidly rocks its body up and down over the pivot point where its legs meet its body.

Ulna–One of two bones supporting the inner wing, corresponding to our own ulna (the long bone on the little-finger side of our forearm).

Underparts–The ventral surface of a bird's body (includes breast, belly, sides, and flanks).

Understory–Those layers of vegetation in the vertical structure of a forest that are below the canopy.

Undertail coverts–Those feathers on the ventral surface of the base of the bird's tail and extending forward to the vent. Also called "crissum."

Upperparts–The dorsal surface of a bird's body (includes back and rump).

Uppertail coverts–Those feathers on the dorsal surface of the base of the bird's tail, posterior to the rump. Not sharply demarcated from the rump, but an imaginary transverse line directly above the vent serves to approximately separate the uppertail coverts from the rump. (Note: The "tail feathers" of a peacock's train are highly modified uppertail coverts, whereas a turkey gobbler's tail fan is comprised of "true" tail feathers, i.e., the flight feathers, or "rectrices," of the tail.)

Vent–The external opening to the cloaca. It is at the posterior margin of the abdomen, and marks the dividing line between the feathers of the abdomen and the undertail coverts. Through it pass fecal matter, urinary wastes, and gonadal products (eggs and sperm).

Ventral–At or toward the bottom.

Wing bar–Contrastingly colored bar on the front part of the inner wing. When the wings are folded, the wing bars rest just behind the shoulder region.

Wing lining–Those feathers on the wing other than the flight feathers.

Wrist–The point on a bird's wing where the radius and ulna join with the metacarpals. Also called the "bend of the wing."

BIBLIOGRAPHY

American Ornithologists' Union. 1983. Check-list of North American birds. 6th ed. Allen Press, Lawrence, KS.

Barbour, R. W., C. T. Peterson, D. Rust, H. E. Shadowen, and A. L. Whitt, Jr. 1973. Kentucky birds: a finding guide. Univ. Press of KY, Lexington.

Bierly, M. L. 1980. Bird finding in Tennessee. M. L. Bierly, Nashville, TN.

Chester, E. W., and W. H. Ellis. 1989. Plant communities of northwestern Middle Tennessee. J. Tenn. Acad. Sci. 64:75-78.

Cornell Laboratory of Ornithology. 1983. A field guide to bird songs of eastern and central North America. 2nd ed. Sound cassettes. Houghton Mifflin Co., Boston, MA.

DeSante, D., and P. Pyle. 1986. Distributional checklist of North American birds. Vol. 1: U.S. and Canada. Artemisia Press, Lee Vining, CA.

Ehrlich, P. R., D. S. Dobkin, and D. Wheye. 1988. The birder's handbook: A field guide to the natural history of North American birds. Simon & Schuster, Inc., New York, NY.

Mengel, R. M. 1965. The birds of Kentucky. American Ornithologists' Union Monograph No. 3. Allen Press, Lawrence, KS.

Monroe, B. L., Jr., A. L. Stamm, and B. L. Palmer-Ball, Jr. 1988. Annotated checklist of the birds of Kentucky. KY Ornithol. Soc., Louisville.

National Geographic Society. 1987. Field guide to the birds of North America. 2nd ed. Nat'l Geogr. Soc., Washington, DC.

Peterson, R. T. 1980. A field guide to the birds of eastern and central North America. 4th ed. Houghton Mifflin Co., Boston, MA.

Robbins, C. S., B. Bruun, and H. S. Zim. 1983. A guide to field identification: birds of North America. Golden Press, New York, NY.

Robinson, J. C. 1990. An annotated checklist of the birds of Tennessee. Univ. of Tenn. Press, Knoxville.

Robinson, J. C. and D. W. Blunk. 1989. The birds of Stewart County, Tennessee. Pp. 70-103 in: Scott, A. F. (ed.), Proceedings of the contributed papers session of the second annual symposium on the natural history of lower Tennessee and Cumberland river valleys. Center for Field Biology of Land Between The Lakes, Austin Peay State University, Clarksville, TN.

INDEX
AND
CHECKLIST OF COMMON NAMES

226

Heron ... (cont'd.)

☐ _____

☐ _____

☐ _____

☐ _____

☐ _____

☐ _____

☐ _____

☐ _____

☐ _____

☐ _____

☐ _____

☐ _____

☐ _____

☐ _____

☐ _____

☐ _____

☐ _____

DAVID H. SNYDER

A native Missourian, David Snyder has been on the faculty of the Department of Biology at Austin Peay State University in Clarksville, Tennessee, since 1962. His interest in birds began in 1957 when he took a course in ornithology under Dr. William H. Elder at the University of Missouri at Columbia. Since then he has pursued birds in much of the U.S., Canada, Mexico, Ecuador, and the Galapagos Islands. David has written one other book, *Amphibians and Reptiles of Land Between The Lakes,* published by Tennessee Valley Authority in 1972. As a professor of biology at APSU he teaches courses in field zoology, ornithology, and evolution. He earned the B.A. and M.A. degrees in wildlife conservation and management at the University of Missouri at Columbia, and a Ph.D. from the University of Notre Dame. He lives with his wife and three youngest children on a 53-acre hardscrabble farm near Palmyra, Tennessee.

FRED J. ALSOP, III

Fred Alsop lives in Johnson City, Tennessee, where he is chairman of the Department of Biological Sciences at East Tennessee State University. An avid birder, Fred has iden-tified more than 2000 species of birds in his travels. As a photographer of birds for more than 20 years, his wildlife pictures have appeared in numerous books and maga-zines. His passion for birds has taken him to all 50 states, throughout Canada, to East Africa, and to many Latin American countries. Fred is author of *Birds of the Smokies*, published by Great Smoky Mountains Natural History Association in 1991. He earned a B.S. degree in biology and fine arts from Austin Peay State University, and an M.S. and Ph.D. from the University of Tennessee at Knoxville. He is a Distinguished Professor at ETSU and serves as a national lecturer for Sigma Xi, The Scientific Research Society.

The Miscellaneous Publications series of **Austin Peay State University's** Center for Field Biology is a medium for disseminating educational, scientific, or technical information which, because of length or content, is not appropriate for scientific journals or as part of the Center's symposium proceedings. Generally papers should relate to the natural history of the lower Cumberland and Tennessee River valleys of Kentucky and Tennessee; however, papers on similar topics from contiguous areas or surrounding states may also be appropriate.

Publications may be obtained from:

Publications Manager
The Center for Field Biology
Austin Peay State University
Clarksville, Tennessee 37044

Make checks payable to **Austin Peay State University**.

Persons interested in publishing in this series should contact the Center's director at the above address.

Papers in the Miscellaneous Publications Series

1. Chester, E. W., R. J. Jensen, L. J. Schibig, and S. Simoni. 1987. The nut trees of Land Between The Lakes.
   (An illustrated guide to the species of beech, chestnut, hickories, oaks, and walnuts of LBL. 49 pp. $3.00 + $1.00 shipping.)
2. Noel, S. M. 1987. A curriculum guide for understanding the woodland community.
   (Student and teacher activities for a unit on woodland ecology. 66 pp. Free to teachers; $3.00 + $1.00 shipping to all others.)
3. Noel, S. M., M. L. McReynolds, and E. W. Chester. 1990. The ferns and fern allies of Land Between The Lakes: a curriculum guide.
   (An illustrated guide with activities for secondary teachers and students. 67 pp. Free to teachers; $3.00 + $1.00 shipping to all others.)
4. Redmond, W. H., A. C. Echternacht, and A. F. Scott. 1990. Annotated checklist and bibliography of amphibians and reptiles of Tennessee (1835 through 1989).
   (A review and update of the information on distributions, taxonomy, and habitats of tennessee's herpetofauna, plus an extensive (1124 titles) annotated list of literature dealing with herpetology in the state. 173 pp. $4.00 + $1.00 shipping.)
5. Snyder, D. H., and F. J. Alsop, III. 1991. Birds of Land Between The Lakes.
   (Accounts of 230 species of birds, with residency status and abundance information, basic descriptions, anecdotal commentaries, and suggestions on how and where to watch birds in the region. Illustrated with 125 color photographs. 234 pp. $7.00 + $1.00 shipping.)

Austin Peay State University is an equal opportunity employer committed to the education of a non-racially identifiable student body. AP-135/5-91/Vaughan/Nash/7M

— Notes —

— Notes —

— Notes —

— Notes —

— Notes —

— Notes —

— Notes —

— Notes —